FUN HOME

A FAMILY TRAGICOMIC

ALISON BECHDEL

HOUGHTON MIFFLIN COMPANY
BOSTON   NEW YORK

FOR MOM, CHRISTIAN, AND JOHN.

WE DID HAVE A LOT OF FUN,
IN SPITE OF EVERYTHING.

COPYRIGHT © 2006 BY ALISON BECHDEL

ALL RIGHTS RESERVED

FOR INFORMATION ABOUT PERMISSION TO REPRODUCE SELECTIONS FROM

THIS BOOK, WRITE TO PERMISSIONS, HOUGHTON MIFFLIN COMPANY,

215 PARK AVENUE SOUTH, NEW YORK, NEW YORK 10003.

VISIT OUR WEB SITE: WWW.HOUGHTONMIFFLINBOOKS.COM

LIBRARY OF CONGRESS CATALOGING-IN-PUBLICATION DATA

BECHDEL, ALISON, DATE.
  FUN HOME : A FAMILY TRAGICOMIC / ALISON BECHDEL.
    P. CM.
  ISBN-13: 978-0-618-47794-4
  ISBN-10: 0-618-47794-2
1. BECHDEL, ALISON, DATE.—COMIC BOOKS, STRIPS, ETC.
2. CARTOONISTS—UNITED STATES—COMIC BOOKS, STRIPS, ETC.
3. GRAPHIC NOVELS. I. TITLE.
  PN6727.B3757Z46 2006
  741.5'973—DC22   2005030304

PRINTED IN THE UNITED STATES OF AMERICA

QWT 10 9 8 7 6 5 4 3 2

CONTENTS

CHAPTER 1

OLD FATHER, OLD ARTIFICER

LIKE MANY FATHERS, MINE COULD OCCASIONALLY BE PREVAILED ON FOR A SPOT OF "AIRPLANE."

AS HE LAUNCHED ME, MY FULL WEIGHT WOULD FALL ON THE PIVOT POINT BETWEEN HIS FEET AND MY STOMACH.

OOF!

IT WAS A DISCOMFORT WELL WORTH THE RARE PHYSICAL CONTACT, AND CERTAINLY WORTH THE MOMENT OF PERFECT BALANCE WHEN I SOARED ABOVE HIM.

IN THE CIRCUS, ACROBATICS WHERE ONE PERSON LIES ON THE FLOOR BALANCING ANOTHER ARE CALLED "ICARIAN GAMES."

3

CONSIDERING THE FATE OF ICARUS AFTER HE FLOUTED HIS FATHER'S ADVICE AND FLEW SO CLOSE TO THE SUN HIS WINGS MELTED, PERHAPS SOME DARK HUMOR IS INTENDED.

UH-OH!

IN OUR PARTICULAR REENACTMENT OF THIS MYTHIC RELATIONSHIP, IT WAS NOT ME BUT MY FATHER WHO WAS TO PLUMMET FROM THE SKY.

BUT BEFORE HE DID SO, HE MANAGED TO GET QUITE A LOT DONE.

AGAIN!

THIS RUG IS FILTHY. GO GET THE VACUUM CLEANER.

HIS GREATEST ACHIEVEMENT, ARGUABLY, WAS HIS MONOMANIACAL RESTORATION OF OUR OLD HOUSE.

AND THEN GET ME MY TACK HAMMER. THAT STRIP OF MOLDING IS LOOSE.

4

WHEN OTHER CHILDREN CALLED OUR HOUSE A MANSION, I WOULD DEMUR. I RESENTED THE IMPLICATION THAT MY FAMILY WAS RICH, OR UNUSUAL IN ANY WAY.

IN FACT, WE WERE UNUSUAL, THOUGH I WOULDN'T APPRECIATE EXACTLY HOW UNUSUAL UNTIL MUCH LATER. BUT WE WERE NOT RICH.

IT'S JUST A HOUSE.

ALISON!

WHAT?

SEND TAMMI HOME. YOU HAVE WORK TO DO.

THE GILT CORNICES, THE MARBLE FIREPLACE, THE CRYSTAL CHANDELIERS, THE SHELVES OF CALF-BOUND BOOKS--THESE WERE NOT SO MUCH BOUGHT AS PRODUCED FROM THIN AIR BY MY FATHER'S REMARKABLE LEGERDEMAIN.

WASH THESE OLD CURTAINS SO WE CAN PUT UP THE HAND-EMBROIDERED LACE ONES I FOUND IN MRS. STRUMP'S ATTIC.

MY FATHER COULD SPIN GARBAGE...

...INTO GOLD.

HE COULD TRANSFIGURE A ROOM WITH THE SMALLEST OFFHAND FLOURISH.

HE COULD CONJURE AN ENTIRE, FINISHED PERIOD INTERIOR FROM A PAINT CHIP.

HE WAS AN ALCHEMIST OF APPEARANCE, A SAVANT OF SURFACE, A DAEDALUS OF DECOR.

FOR IF MY FATHER WAS ICARUS, HE WAS ALSO DAEDALUS--THAT SKILLFUL ARTIFICER, THAT MAD SCIENTIST WHO BUILT THE WINGS FOR HIS SON AND DESIGNED THE FAMOUS LABYRINTH...

THIS IS THE WALLPAPER FOR MY ROOM?

...AND WHO ANSWERED NOT TO THE LAWS OF SOCIETY, BUT TO THOSE OF HIS CRAFT.

BUT I **HATE** PINK! I **HATE** FLOWERS!

TOUGH TITTY.

HISTORICAL RESTORATION WASN'T HIS JOB.

(TWELFTH-GRADE ENGLISH)

ARCHI-TECTURAL DIGEST

IT WAS HIS PASSION. AND I MEAN PASSION IN EVERY SENSE OF THE WORD.

LIBIDINAL. MANIC. MARTYRED.

OUR GOTHIC REVIVAL HOUSE HAD BEEN BUILT DURING THE SMALL PENNSYLVANIA TOWN'S ONE BRIEF MOMENT OF WEALTH, FROM THE LUMBER INDUSTRY, IN 1867.

BUT LOCAL FORTUNES HAD DECLINED STEADILY FROM THAT POINT, AND WHEN MY PARENTS BOUGHT THE PLACE IN 1962, IT WAS A SHELL OF ITS FORMER SELF.

THE SHUTTERS AND SCROLLWORK WERE GONE. THE CLAPBOARDS HAD BEEN SHEATHED WITH SCABROUS SHINGLES.

THE BARE LIGHTBULBS REVEALED DINGY WARTIME WALLPAPER AND WOODWORK PAINTED PASTEL GREEN.

ALL THAT WAS LEFT OF THE HOUSE'S LUMBER-ERA GLORY WERE THE EXUBERANT FRONT PORCH SUPPORTS.

BUT OVER THE NEXT EIGHTEEN YEARS, MY FATHER WOULD RESTORE THE HOUSE TO ITS ORIGINAL CONDITION, AND THEN SOME.

JESUS! THIS MUST BE THE PATTERN FOR THE ORIGINAL BARGEBOARD!

HE WOULD PERFORM, AS DAEDALUS DID, DAZZLING DISPLAYS OF ARTFULNESS.

HE WOULD CULTIVATE THE BARREN YARD...   ...INTO A LUSH, FLOWERING LANDSCAPE.

HE WOULD MANIPULATE FLAGSTONES
THAT WEIGHED HALF A TON...

...AND THE THINNEST, QUIVERING LAYERS
OF GOLD LEAF.

IT COULD
HAVE BEEN
A ROMANTIC
STORY, LIKE
IN *IT'S A
WONDERFUL
LIFE*, WHEN
JIMMY STEWART
AND DONNA
REED FIX UP
THAT BIG OLD
HOUSE AND
RAISE THEIR
FAMILY THERE.

Merry Christmas

HELLO, DARLING!

HELLO, DADDY!

10

BUT IN THE MOVIE WHEN JIMMY STEWART COMES HOME ONE NIGHT AND STARTS YELLING AT EVERYONE...

...IT'S OUT OF THE ORDINARY.

DAEDALUS, TOO, WAS INDIFFERENT TO THE HUMAN COST OF HIS PROJECTS.

HE BLITHELY BETRAYED THE KING, FOR EXAMPLE, WHEN THE QUEEN ASKED HIM TO BUILD HER A COW DISGUISE SO SHE COULD SEDUCE THE WHITE BULL.

INDEED, THE RESULT OF THAT SCHEME--A HALF-BULL, HALF-MAN MONSTER--INSPIRED DAEDALUS'S GREATEST CREATION YET.

HE HID THE MINOTAUR IN THE LABYRINTH-- A MAZE OF PASSAGES AND ROOMS OPEN- ING ENDLESSLY INTO ONE ANOTHER...

...AND FROM WHICH, AS STRAY YOUTHS AND MAIDENS DISCOVERED TO THEIR PERIL...

...ESCAPE WAS IMPOSSIBLE.

THEN THERE ARE THOSE FAMOUS WINGS. WAS DAEDALUS REALLY STRICKEN WITH GRIEF WHEN ICARUS FELL INTO THE SEA?

OR JUST DISAPPOINTED BY THE DESIGN FAILURE?

SOMETIMES, WHEN THINGS WERE GOING WELL, I THINK MY FATHER ACTUALLY ENJOYED HAVING A FAMILY.

AND OF COURSE, MY BROTHERS AND I WERE FREE LABOR. DAD CONSIDERED US EXTENSIONS OF HIS OWN BODY, LIKE PRECISION ROBOT ARMS.

OR AT LEAST, THE AIR OF AUTHENTICITY WE LENT TO HIS EXHIBIT. A SORT OF STILL LIFE WITH CHILDREN.

PUT HOT, SOAPY WATER IN THE SINK AND GET SOME CLEAN RAGS.

IN THIS REGARD, IT WAS LIKE BEING RAISED NOT BY JIMMY BUT BY MARTHA STEWART.

IN THEORY, HIS ARRANGEMENT WITH MY MOTHER WAS MORE COOPERATIVE.

WHAT DO YOU THINK OF THIS GAS CHANDELIER?

BORDELLO.

AUCTION CATALOG

IN PRACTICE, IT WAS NOT.

13

WE EACH RESISTED IN OUR OWN WAYS, BUT IN THE END WE WERE EQUALLY POWERLESS BEFORE MY FATHER'S CURATORIAL ONSLAUGHT.

WHOREHOUSE.

IT'S HIDEOUS.

EH-EH-EH-EH! PKRGH!

IT LOOKS LIKE SKULLS.

MY BROTHERS AND I COULDN'T COMPETE WITH THE ASTRAL LAMPS AND GIRANDOLES AND HEPPLEWHITE SUITE CHAIRS. THEY WERE PERFECT.

GET YOUR STINKIN' FEET AWAY FROM ME.

ALISON, COME HELP ME HANG THIS MIRROR IN YOUR ROOM.

I GREW TO RESENT THE WAY MY FATHER TREATED HIS FURNITURE LIKE CHILDREN, AND HIS CHILDREN LIKE FURNITURE.

MY OWN DECIDED PREFERENCE FOR THE UNADORNED AND PURELY FUNCTIONAL EMERGED EARLY.

HOLD IT HIGHER. DON'T MOVE.

I HATE THIS ROOM.

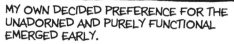

WHEN I GROW UP, MY HOUSE IS GOING TO BE ALL METAL, LIKE A SUBMARINE.

I WAS SPARTAN TO MY FATHER'S ATHENIAN. MODERN TO HIS VICTORIAN.

BUTCH TO HIS NELLY. UTILITARIAN TO HIS AESTHETE.

I DEVELOPED A CONTEMPT FOR USE-LESS ORNAMENT. WHAT FUNCTION WAS SERVED BY THE SCROLLS, TASSELS, AND BRIC-A-BRAC THAT INFESTED OUR HOUSE?

IF ANYTHING, THEY OBSCURED FUNCTION. THEY WERE EMBELLISHMENTS IN THE WORST SENSE.

PLING
KLINK

THEY WERE LIES.

INCIPIENT YELLOW LUNG DISEASE

MY FATHER BEGAN TO SEEM MORALLY SUSPECT TO ME LONG BEFORE I KNEW THAT HE ACTUALLY HAD A DARK SECRET.

MOM SAYS HURRY UP.

"BRONZING STICK"

HE USED HIS SKILLFUL ARTIFICE NOT TO MAKE THINGS, BUT TO MAKE THINGS APPEAR TO BE WHAT THEY WERE NOT.

MASS WILL BE OVER BEFORE WE GET THERE.

THAT IS TO SAY, IMPECCABLE.

HE APPEARED TO BE AN IDEAL HUSBAND AND FATHER, FOR EXAMPLE.

IT'S TEMPTING TO SUGGEST, IN RETRO-SPECT, THAT OUR FAMILY WAS A SHAM.

THAT OUR HOUSE WAS NOT A REAL HOME AT ALL BUT THE SIMULACRUM OF ONE, A MUSEUM.

YET WE REALLY WERE A FAMILY, AND WE REALLY DID LIVE IN THOSE PERIOD ROOMS.

STILL, SOMETHING VITAL WAS MISSING.

WELL?

ME, AGE 4

MY BROTHER CHRISTIAN, AGE 3

BUT I DIDN'T DO ANYTHING!

AN ELASTICITY, A MARGIN FOR ERROR.

HOW DID THIS VASE GET SO CLOSE TO THE EDGE OF THE TABLE?

MOST PEOPLE, I IMAGINE, LEARN TO ACCEPT THAT THEY'RE NOT PERFECT.

BUT AN IDLE REMARK ABOUT MY FATHER'S TIE OVER BREAKFAST COULD SEND HIM INTO A TAILSPIN.

PEACE, MAN.

MY MOTHER ESTABLISHED A RULE.

DON'T CHANGE IT! WE'RE LATE!

ALSO AN ENGLISH TEACHER

NO COMMENTS ON HIS APPEARANCE. IS THAT UNDERSTOOD?

WHAT IF IT'S SOMETHING GOOD?

GOOD, BAD, IT DOESN'T MATTER.

IF WE COULDN'T CRITICIZE MY FATHER, SHOWING AFFECTION FOR HIM WAS AN EVEN DICIER VENTURE.

WE WERE NOT A PHYSICALLY EXPRESSIVE FAMILY, TO SAY THE LEAST. BUT ONCE I WAS UNACCOUNTABLY MOVED TO KISS MY FATHER GOOD NIGHT.

HAVING LITTLE PRACTICE WITH THE GESTURE, ALL I MANAGED WAS TO GRAB HIS HAND AND BUSS THE KNUCKLES LIGHTLY...

...AS IF HE WERE A BISHOP OR AN ELEGANT LADY, BEFORE RUSHING FROM THE ROOM IN EMBARRASSMENT.

19

THIS EMBARRASSMENT ON MY PART WAS A TINY SCALE MODEL OF MY FATHER'S MORE FULLY DEVELOPED SELF-LOATHING.

HIS SHAME INHABITED OUR HOUSE AS PERVASIVELY AND INVISIBLY AS THE AROMATIC MUSK OF AGING MAHOGANY.

IN FACT, THE METICULOUS, PERIOD INTERIORS WERE EXPRESSLY DESIGNED TO CONCEAL IT.

MIRRORS, DISTRACTING BRONZES, MULTIPLE DOORWAYS. VISITORS OFTEN GOT LOST UPSTAIRS.

GRACIOUS, I ALMOST WALKED RIGHT INTO THIS!

MY MOTHER, MY BROTHERS, AND I KNEW OUR WAY AROUND WELL ENOUGH, BUT IT WAS IMPOSSIBLE TO TELL IF THE MINOTAUR LAY BEYOND THE NEXT CORNER.

AND THE CONSTANT TENSION WAS HEIGHT-ENED BY THE FACT THAT SOME ENCOUNTERS COULD BE QUITE PLEASANT.

HIS BURSTS OF KINDNESS WERE AS INCANDESCENT AS HIS TANTRUMS WERE DARK.

ALTHOUGH I'M GOOD AT ENUMERATING MY FATHER'S FLAWS, IT'S HARD FOR ME TO SUSTAIN MUCH ANGER AT HIM.

I EXPECT THIS IS PARTLY BECAUSE HE'S DEAD, AND PARTLY BECAUSE THE BAR IS LOWER FOR FATHERS THAN FOR MOTHERS.

STOP SPLASHING!

IN MY EYES!

HOLD STILL, DAMMIT!

MY MOTHER MUST HAVE BATHED ME HUNDREDS OF TIMES. BUT IT'S MY FATHER RINSING ME OFF WITH THE PURPLE METAL CUP THAT I REMEMBER MOST CLEARLY.

THE SUFFUSION OF WARMTH AS THE HOT WATER SLUICED OVER ME...

...THE SUDDEN, UNBEARABLE COLD OF ITS ABSENCE.

WAS HE A GOOD FATHER? I WANT TO SAY, "AT LEAST HE STUCK AROUND." BUT OF COURSE, HE DIDN'T.

AGAIN!

IT'S TRUE THAT HE DIDN'T KILL HIMSELF UNTIL I WAS NEARLY TWENTY.

BUT HIS ABSENCE RESONATED RETRO-ACTIVELY, ECHOING BACK THROUGH ALL THE TIME I KNEW HIM.

MAYBE IT WAS THE CONVERSE OF THE WAY AMPUTEES FEEL PAIN IN A MISSING LIMB.

HE REALLY WAS THERE ALL THOSE YEARS, A FLESH-AND-BLOOD PRESENCE STEAMING OFF THE WALLPAPER, DIGGING UP THE DOGWOODS, POLISHING THE FINIALS...

...SMELLING OF SAWDUST AND SWEAT AND DESIGNER COLOGNE.

BUT I ACHED AS IF HE WERE ALREADY GONE.

23

CHAPTER 2

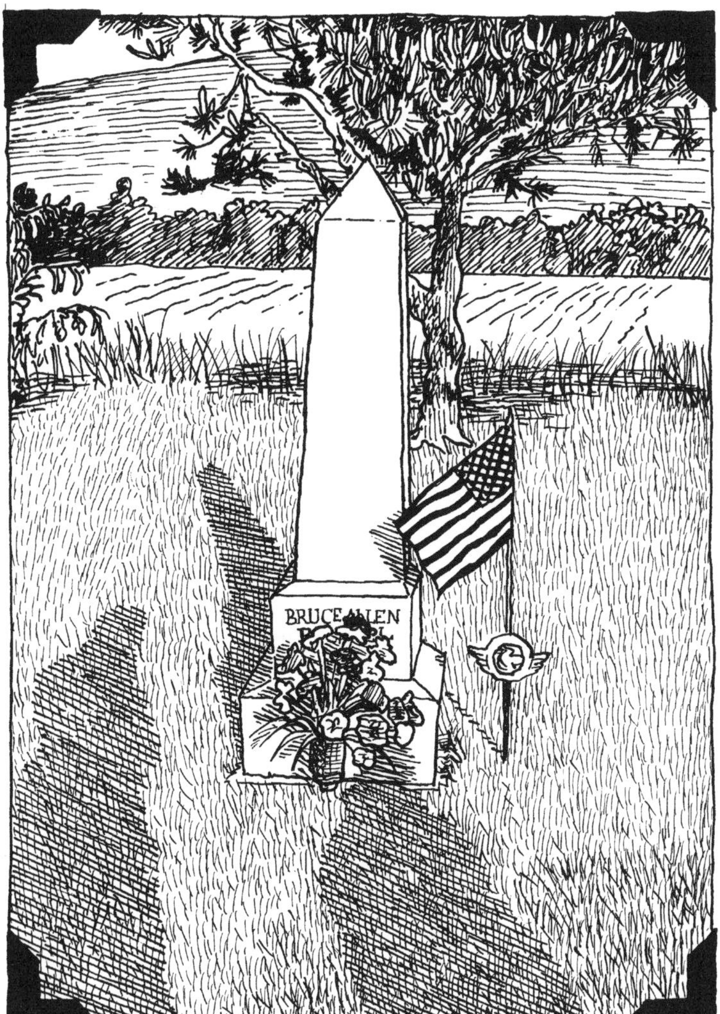
BRUCE ALLEN

A HAPPY DEATH

THERE'S NO PROOF, ACTUALLY, THAT MY FATHER KILLED HIMSELF.

NO ONE KNEW IT WASN'T AN ACCIDENT.

HIS DEATH WAS QUITE POSSIBLY HIS CONSUMMATE ARTIFICE, HIS MASTERSTROKE.

I CAN'T BELIEVE IT. SUCH A GOOD MAN.

THERE'S NO PROOF, BUT THERE ARE SOME SUGGESTIVE CIRCUMSTANCES. THE FACT THAT MY MOTHER HAD ASKED HIM FOR A DIVORCE TWO WEEKS BEFORE.

SUCH A GOOD MAN.

THE COPY OF CAMUS' *A HAPPY DEATH* THAT HE'D BEEN READING AND LEAVING AROUND THE HOUSE IN WHAT MIGHT BE CONSTRUED AS A DELIBERATE MANNER.

CAMUS' FIRST NOVEL, IT'S ABOUT A CONSUMPTIVE HERO WHO DOES NOT DIE A PARTICULARLY HAPPY DEATH. MY FATHER HAD HIGHLIGHTED ONE LINE.

BUT DAD WAS ALWAYS READING SOMETHING. SHOULD WE HAVE BEEN SUSPICIOUS WHEN HE STARTED PLOWING THROUGH PROUST THE YEAR BEFORE?

spared him a great deal of loneliness. He had been unfair: while his imagination and vanity had given her too much importance, his pride had given her too little. He discovered the cruel paradox by which we always deceive ourselves twice about the people we love – first to their advantage, then to their disadvantage. Today he understood that Marthe had been genuine with him– that she had been what she was, and that he owed her a good deal. It was beginning to ra... s of the street; t... aw Marthe's sudd... by a burst of gratitude he could not express– in the old

A FITTING EPITAPH FOR MY PARENTS' MARRIAGE.

WAS THAT A SIGN OF DESPERATION? IT'S SAID, AFTER ALL, THAT PEOPLE REACH MIDDLE AGE THE DAY THEY REALIZE THEY'RE NEVER GOING TO READ *REMEMBRANCE OF THINGS PAST*. DAD ALSO LEFT A MARGINAL NOTATION IN ANOTHER BOOK.

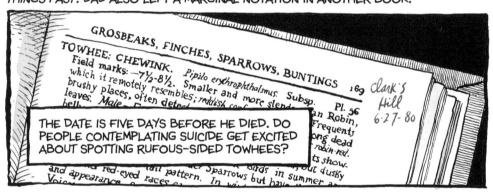

GROSBEAKS, FINCHES, SPARROWS, BUNTINGS 169

TOWHEE: CHEWINK. *Pipilo erythrophthalmus.* Subsp.
Field marks:—7½–8½. Smaller and more slend...
which it remotely resembles; reddish...
brushy places, often detec...
leaves. Male...

Clark's Hill 6·27·80

THE DATE IS FIVE DAYS BEFORE HE DIED. DO PEOPLE CONTEMPLATING SUICIDE GET EXCITED ABOUT SPOTTING RUFOUS–SIDED TOWHEES?

MAYBE HE DIDN'T NOTICE THE TRUCK COMING BECAUSE HE WAS PREOCCUPIED WITH THE DIVORCE. PEOPLE OFTEN HAVE ACCIDENTS WHEN THEY'RE DISTRAUGHT.

BUT THESE ARE JUST QUIBBLES. I DON'T BELIEVE IT WAS AN ACCIDENT.

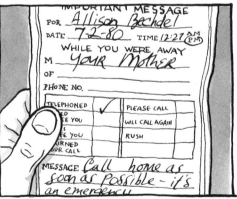

IMPORTANT MESSAGE
FOR Allison Bechdel
DATE 7-2-80 TIME 12:27 AM PM
WHILE YOU WERE AWAY
M Your Mother
OF
PHONE NO.
TELEPHONED ✓ | PLEASE CALL
...E YOU | WILL CALL AGAIN
...E YOU | RUSH
...URNED
...UR CALL
MESSAGE Call home as soon as possible – it's an emergency

AFTER I HAD MADE THE FIVE-HOUR DRIVE HOME FROM COLLEGE AND EVERYONE ELSE HAD GONE TO BED, MOM AND I DISCUSSED IT.

IT'S POSSIBLE THAT WE CHOSE TO BELIEVE THIS BECAUSE IT WAS LESS PAINFUL.

IF HE'D INTENDED TO DIE, THERE WAS A CERTAIN CONSOLATION IN THE FACT THAT HE SUCCEEDED WITH SUCH APLOMB.

I THINK IT WAS SOMETHING HE ALWAYS MEANT TO DO.

HIS HEADSTONE IS AN OBELISK, A STRIKING ANACHRONISM AMONG THE UNGAINLY GRANITE SLABS IN THE NEW END OF THE CEMETERY.

IT'S ALSO A SHAPE THAT IN LIFE HE WAS UNABASHEDLY FIXATED ON.

HE HAD AN OBELISK COLLECTION, IN FACT, AND HIS PRIZE SPECIMEN WAS ONE IN KNEE-HIGH JADE THAT PROPPED OPEN THE DOOR TO HIS LIBRARY.

IT SYMBOLIZES LIFE.

29

HIS ULTIMATE OBELISK IS NOT CARVED FROM FLESHY, TRANSLUCENT MARBLE LIKE THE TOMBSTONES IN THE OLD PART OF THE CEMETERY.

MOM COULDN'T CONVINCE THE MONUMENT MAKER TO DO IT.

IT WON'T LAST. IN TEN, TWENTY YEARS YOU'LL HAVE LICHEN, EROSION. TRUST ME, YOU WANT GRANITE.

STRECK Monuments

THE GRANITE IS HANDSOME, CRISP... AND, WELL, LIFELESS.

ANNA FEARON
Daughter
Wᵐ & BEULAH TEMPLE
Born Jan. 20, 1782
Died
Nov. 4, 1870
Aged
88ly. 9 mos.

BRUCE ALLEN BECHDEL 1936 — 1980

ON A MAP OF MY HOMETOWN, A CIRCLE A MILE AND A HALF IN DIAMETER CIRCUMSCRIBES:

(A) DAD'S GRAVE,

(B) THE SPOT ON ROUTE 150 WHERE HE DIED, NEAR AN OLD FARMHOUSE HE WAS RESTORING,

(C) THE HOUSE WHERE HE AND MY MOTHER RAISED OUR FAMILY, AND

(D) THE FARM WHERE HE WAS BORN.

THIS NARROW COMPASS SUGGESTS A PROVINCIALISM ON MY FATHER'S PART THAT IS BOTH MISLEADING AND ACCURATE.

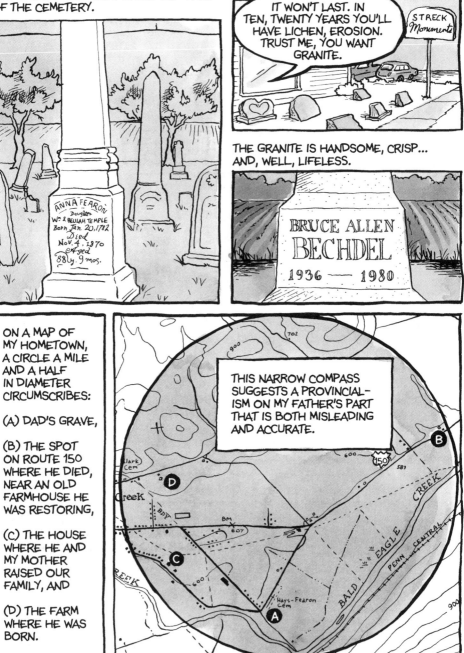

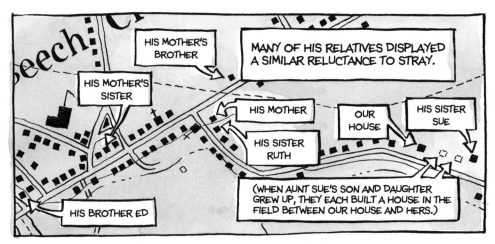

BUT IT'S PUZZLING WHY MY URBANE FATHER, WITH HIS UNWHOLESOME INTEREST IN THE DECORATIVE ARTS, REMAINED IN THIS PROVINCIAL HAMLET.

AND WHY MY CULTURED MOTHER, WHO HAD STUDIED ACTING IN NEW YORK CITY, WOULD LIVE THERE CHEEK BY JOWL WITH HIS FAMILY IS MORE PUZZLING STILL.

IT WAS MADE CLEAR THAT MY BROTHERS AND I WOULD NOT REPEAT THEIR MISTAKE.

31

MY PARENTS HAD IN FACT GOTTEN AS FAR AS EUROPE, WHERE MY FATHER WAS STATIONED IN THE ARMY. MOM FLEW THERE TO MARRY HIM.

THEY LIVED IN WEST GERMANY FOR ALMOST A YEAR DURING DAD'S SERVICE, IN SOME DEGREE OF EXPATRIATE SPLENDOR.

A LOCAL

THE TIN DRUM

BUT THEN, THE STORY GOES, MY GRANDFATHER HAD A HEART ATTACK AND DAD HAD TO GO HOME AND RUN THE FAMILY BUSINESS.

PREGNANT WITH ME

BECHDEL? YOU JUST GOT A MESSAGE FROM YOUR SISTER. CALL HOME ASAP.

THIS WAS A FUNERAL PARLOR BEGUN BY MY GREAT-GRANDFATHER, EDGAR T. BECHDEL.

MY GREAT-GRANDFATHER

MY GRANDFATHER

THE FIRST AUTO HEARSE, 1922

BECHDEL

THE CHANGE IN PLANS WAS A CRUEL BLOW. I WAS BORN SOON AFTER THEY GOT BACK.

FOR A SHORT TIME WE ALL LIVED WITH MY GRANDMOTHER AND AILING GRANDFATHER AT THE FUNERAL HOME.

LESS THAN A YEAR LATER, WE MOVED TO A RENTED FEDERAL-STYLE FARMHOUSE AND MY BROTHER CHRISTIAN WAS BORN.

DAD STARTED TEACHING HIGH SCHOOL ENGLISH. FUNERAL DIRECTING PROVIDED ONLY A PART-TIME INCOME IN OUR THINLY POPULATED REGION.

BY THE TIME WE MOVED TO THE GOTHIC REVIVAL HOUSE AND JOHN WAS BORN, EUROPE HAD DISAPPEARED FROM MY PARENTS' HORIZON.

IT WAS SOMEWHERE DURING THOSE EARLY YEARS THAT I BEGAN CONFUSING US WITH THE ADDAMS FAMILY.

LONG BEFORE I COULD READ, I WOULD PUZZLE OVER A BOOK OF ADDAMS CARTOONS.

THE CAPTIONS ELUDED ME, AS DID THE IRONIC REVERSAL OF SUBURBAN CONFORMITY. HERE WERE THE FAMILIAR DARK, LOFTY CEILINGS, PEELING WALLPAPER, AND MENACING HORSEHAIR FURNISHINGS OF MY OWN HOME.

IN ONE OCCULT AND WORDLESS CARTOON...

...A WORRIED GIRL HAD A STRING RUNNING FROM HER MOUTH TO A TRAP DOOR.

THE LAMP NEXT TO HER LOOKED JUST LIKE MY LAMP. IN FACT, THE GIRL LOOKED JUST LIKE ME.

THE RESEMBLANCE IN MY FIRST-GRADE SCHOOL PHOTO IS EERIE.

WEARING A BLACK VELVET DRESS MY FATHER HAD WRESTLED ME INTO, I APPEAR TO BE IN MOURNING.

MY MOTHER, WITH HER LUXURIANT BLACK HAIR AND PALE SKIN, BORE A MORE THAN PASSING LIKENESS TO MORTICIA.

MOM, HOW COME YOU NEVER GO OUTSIDE?

I TOLD YOU, I'M A VAMPIRE.

NOCTURNE

AND ON WARM SUMMER NIGHTS, IT WAS NOT UNUSUAL FOR A BAT TO SWOOP THROUGH OUR LIVING ROOM.

BUT WHAT GAVE THE COMPARISON REAL WEIGHT WAS THE FAMILY BUSINESS...

...AND THE CAVALIER ATTITUDE WHICH, INEVITABLY, WE CAME TO TAKE TOWARD IT.

CAN I GET IN?

THE "FUN HOME," AS WE CALLED IT, WAS UP ON MAIN STREET.

MY GRANDMOTHER LIVED IN THE FRONT. THE BUSINESS WAS IN THE BACK.

I REMEMBER SEEING MY GRANDFATHER LAID OUT THERE WHEN I WAS THREE. PEOPLE WERE AMUSED BY WHAT SEEMED TO ME A REASONABLE ENOUGH REQUEST.

PUT ME CLOSER.

MY FATHER HAD BEEN GIVEN A FREE HAND WITH THE INTERIOR DECORATION OF THE VIEWING AREA, AND THE ROOMS WERE HUNG WITH DARK VELVET DRAPERY. THIS ENSURED A SOMBER MOOD ON THE SUNNIEST OF DAYS.

THERE WAS A MINIMUM OF FURNITURE, AND A VAST EXPANSE OF TEXTURED OLIVE WALL-TO-WALL CARPETING.

MY BROTHERS AND I HAD LOTS OF CHORES AT THE FUN HOME, BUT ALSO MANY INTERESTING OPPORTUNITIES FOR PLAY.

WE WERE STRICTLY FORBIDDEN TO CLIMB INTO THE CASKETS.

AND THE CRUSHABLE CAPSULES FILLED WITH SMELLING SALTS.

THESE WERE FOR REVIVING PEOPLE WHEN THEY FAINTED FROM SHOCK OR GRIEF, WHICH, DISAPPOINTINGLY, NEVER SEEMED TO HAPPEN.

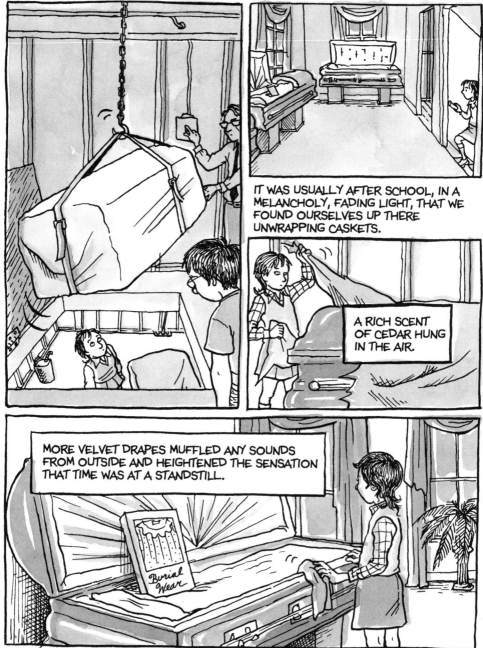

WHEN A NEW SHIPMENT OF CASKETS CAME IN, WE'D LIFT THEM WITH A WINCH TO THE SHOWROOM ON THE SECOND FLOOR OF THE GARAGE.

THOUGH THERE WERE NEVER ANY DEAD PEOPLE IN THE SHOWROOM, IT HAD THE OTHERWORLDLY AMBIENCE OF A MAUSOLEUM.

IT WAS USUALLY AFTER SCHOOL, IN A MELANCHOLY, FADING LIGHT, THAT WE FOUND OURSELVES UP THERE UNWRAPPING CASKETS.

A RICH SCENT OF CEDAR HUNG IN THE AIR.

MORE VELVET DRAPES MUFFLED ANY SOUNDS FROM OUTSIDE AND HEIGHTENED THE SENSATION THAT TIME WAS AT A STANDSTILL.

Burial Wear

LIKE A MEDIUM CHANNELING LOST SOULS, THE FILAMENT OF A SPACE HEATER VIBRATED TUNELESSLY TO OUR FOOTFALLS.

IT WASN'T THE SORT OF PLACE YOU WANTED TO BE ALONE IN.

WAIT FOR ME!

ON THE OTHER HAND, IT WAS NOT PARTICULARLY SCARY TO SPEND THE NIGHT IN THE FUNERAL HOME PROPER, EVEN WHEN WE HAD A DEAD PERSON.

MY BROTHERS AND I OFTEN SLEPT THERE WITH MY GRANDMOTHER.

PERMANENT GREASE STAIN FROM MY DEAD GRANDFATHER'S VITALIS

TO QUIET US DOWN, GRAMMY WOULD LET US SWEEP THE CEILING WITH THE BEAM OF HER FLASHLIGHT IN SEARCH OF BUGS.

THERE'S ONE!

PISS-ANT!

WHEN WE SPOTTED ONE, SHE WOULD DECLARE IT TO BE EITHER A "PISS-ANT" OR AN "ANTIE-MIRE"-- A TAXONOMIC DIFFERENTIATION I WAS NEVER CLEAR ON--AND SQUASH IT WITH A RAG ON THE END OF A BROOM.

AFTER THIS, WE WOULD BEG HER TO TELL US A STORY.

THE STORY, I SHOULD SAY, BECAUSE THERE WAS ONE TALE THAT HELD US IN SUCH THRALL THAT THE REST OF MY GRANDMOTHER'S REPERTOIRE--HER STILLBORN TWINS, THE TIME MY AUNT HAD WORMS--PALED BEFORE IT.

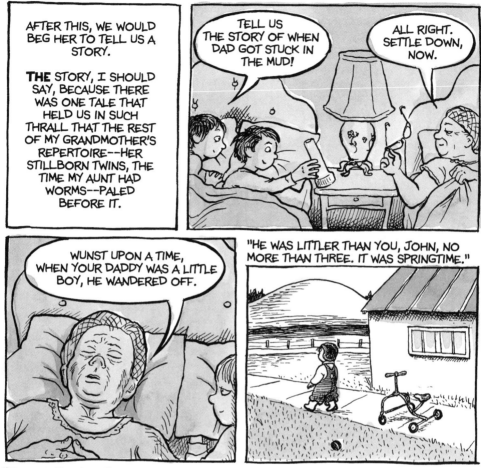

TELL US THE STORY OF WHEN DAD GOT STUCK IN THE MUD!

ALL RIGHT. SETTLE DOWN, NOW.

WUNST UPON A TIME, WHEN YOUR DADDY WAS A LITTLE BOY, HE WANDERED OFF.

"HE WAS LITTLER THAN YOU, JOHN, NO MORE THAN THREE. IT WAS SPRINGTIME."

"THE FIELDS WAS JUST PLOWED, AND BRUCE LIT OUT ACROST ONE. IT WAS THAT WET, PRETTY SOON HE COULDN'T LIFT HIS LITTLE LEGS OUT OF THE MUD!"

40

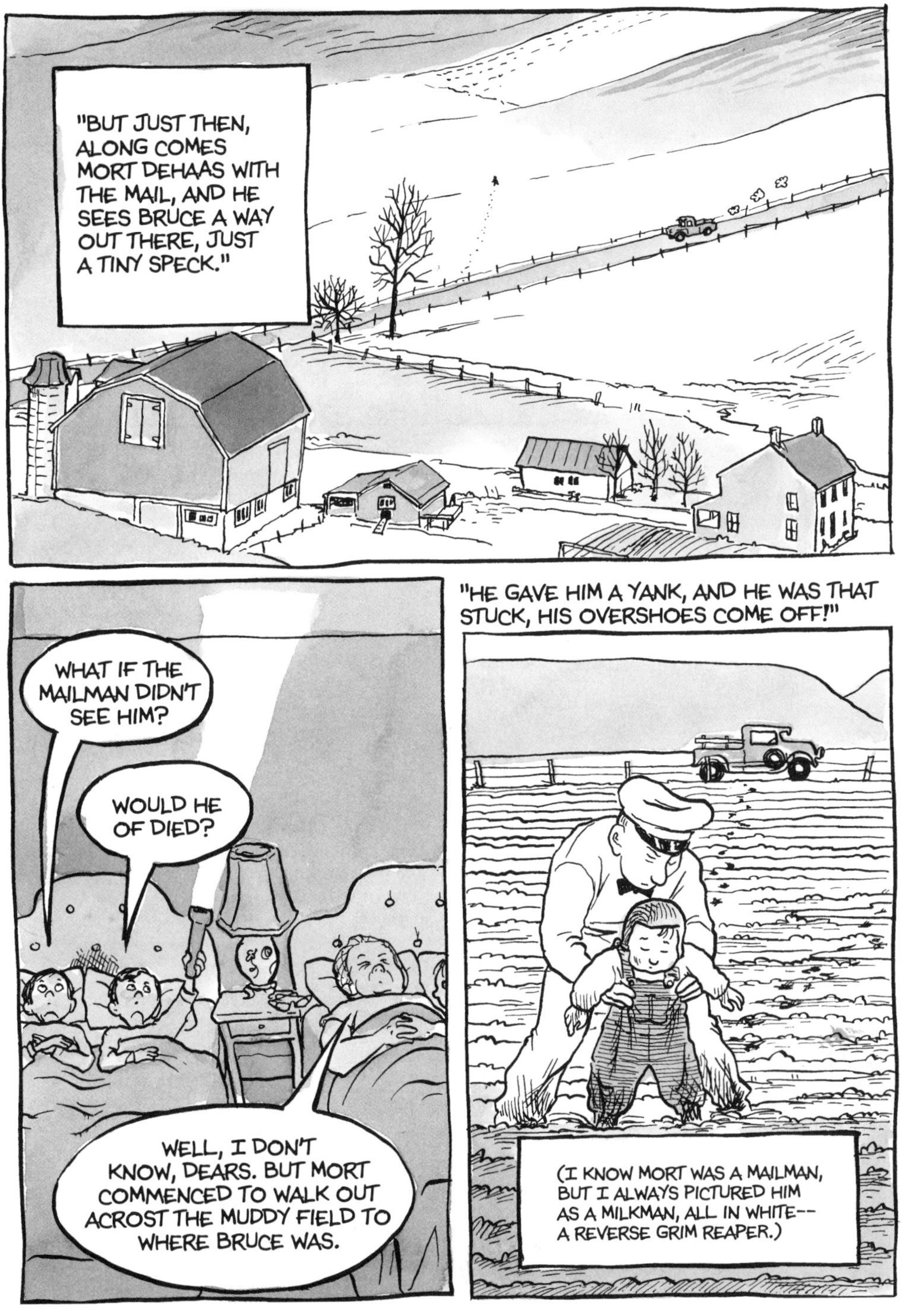
"BUT JUST THEN, ALONG COMES MORT DEHAAS WITH THE MAIL, AND HE SEES BRUCE A WAY OUT THERE, JUST A TINY SPECK."
WHAT IF THE MAILMAN DIDN'T SEE HIM?
WOULD HE OF DIED?
WELL, I DON'T KNOW, DEARS. BUT MORT COMMENCED TO WALK OUT ACROST THE MUDDY FIELD TO WHERE BRUCE WAS.
"HE GAVE HIM A YANK, AND HE WAS THAT STUCK, HIS OVERSHOES COME OFF!"
(I KNOW MORT WAS A MAILMAN, BUT I ALWAYS PICTURED HIM AS A MILKMAN, ALL IN WHITE-- A REVERSE GRIM REAPER.)

"HE BRUNG YOUR DADDY INTO THE KITCHEN IN HIS STOCKING FEET, AND I UNDRESSED HIM RIGHT THERE."

LOSE SOMETHIN', DOROTHY?

OH, MY LANDS!

UNDRESSED HIM?!

WHY?

WHY, HE WAS ALL OVER MUD, DEARS.

THEN WHAT?!

AND HERE THE STORY REACHED ITS BIZARRE, GRIMMSIAN CLIMAX.

THEN I WRAPPED HIM IN A QUILT AND PUT HIM IN THE OVEN.

SHE WAS REFERRING, OF COURSE, TO A COOK-STOVE.

BUT ALL WE COULD ENVISION WAS THE MODERN OVEN SHE HAD NOW, WITH ITS RED-HOT ELEMENTS.

THE TALE WAS ENDLESSLY COMPELLING.

AGAIN!

WUNST MORE, THEN WE'LL GO TO SLEEP.

BY DAY, IT WAS DIFFICULT TO IMAGINE DAD EVER HELPLESS, NAKED, OR TRUSSED UP IN THE OVEN.

WHEN YOU'RE DONE, DO THE VACUUMING.

THAT'S CHRISTIAN'S JOB.

THOUGH THE WAY GRAMMY HELPED HIM TIE HIS SURGICAL GOWN IN BACK WAS EVOCATIVE.

DO IT, OR I'LL GIVE YOU SOMETHING TO WHINE ABOUT.

DAD WORKED BACK IN THE INNER SANCTUM, THE EMBALMING ROOM.

PRIVATE

THIS SMELLED OF BACTERICIDAL SOAP AND EMBALMING FLUID. IT WAS DOMINATED BY A PORCELAIN ENAMEL PREP TABLE AND A CURIOUS WALL CHART.

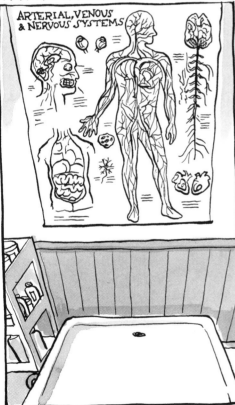

ARTERIAL, VENOUS & NERVOUS SYSTEMS

I DIDN'T NORMALLY SEE THE BODIES BEFORE THEY WERE DRESSED AND IN A CASKET.

ALISON!

BUT ONE DAY DAD CALLED ME BACK THERE.

THE MAN ON THE PREP TABLE WAS BEARDED AND FLESHY, JARRINGLY UNLIKE DAD'S USUAL TRAFFIC OF DESSICATED OLD PEOPLE.

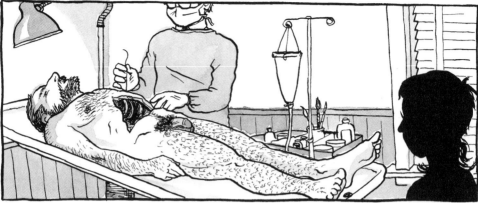

THE STRANGE PILE OF HIS GENITALS WAS SHOCKING, BUT WHAT REALLY GOT MY ATTENTION WAS HIS CHEST, SPLIT OPEN TO A DARK RED CAVE.

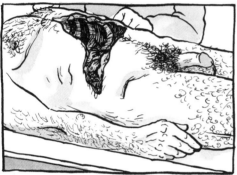

THERE WAS SOME PRACTICAL EXCHANGE WITH MY FATHER DURING WHICH I STUDIOUSLY BETRAYED NO EMOTION.

HAND ME THOSE SCISSORS OVER BY THE SINK.

IT FELT LIKE A TEST. MAYBE THIS WAS THE SAME OFFHANDED WAY HIS OWN NOTORIOUSLY COLD FATHER HAD SHOWN HIM **HIS** FIRST CADAVER.

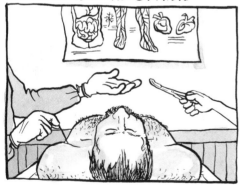

OR MAYBE HE FELT THAT HE'D BECOME TOO INURED TO DEATH, AND WAS HOPING TO ELICIT FROM ME AN EXPRESSION OF THE NATURAL HORROR HE WAS NO LONGER CAPABLE OF.

OR MAYBE HE JUST NEEDED THE SCISSORS.

IS THAT ALL?

MM–HMM.

I HAVE MADE USE OF THE FORMER TECH-NIQUE MYSELF, HOWEVER, THIS ATTEMPT TO ACCESS EMOTION VICARIOUSLY.

PRIVATE

FOR YEARS AFTER MY FATHER'S DEATH, WHEN THE SUBJECT OF PARENTS CAME UP IN CONVERSATION I WOULD RELATE THE INFORMATION IN A FLAT, MATTER-OF-FACT TONE...

MY DAD'S DEAD. HE JUMPED IN FRONT OF A TRUCK.

...EAGER TO DETECT IN MY LISTENER THE FLINCH OF GRIEF THAT ELUDED ME.

MI-CHINITA CUBAN-CHINI

WALK

DONT WALK

THE EMOTION I HAD SUPPRESSED FOR THE GAPING CADAVER SEEMED TO STAY SUPPRESSED.

EVEN WHEN IT WAS DAD HIMSELF ON THE PREP TABLE.

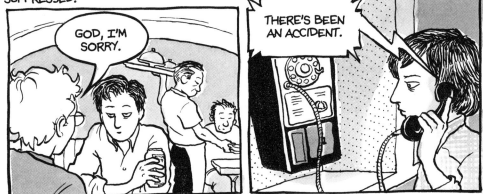

GOD, I'M SORRY.

THERE'S BEEN AN ACCIDENT.

I WAS AWAY AT SCHOOL THAT SUMMER, GENERATING BAR CODES FOR ALL THE BOOKS IN THE COLLEGE LIBRARY.

I HAVE TO GO HOME. MY FATHER GOT HIT BY A TRUCK.

PRIMITIVE MODEM

OH MY GOD. IS HE OKAY?

UMM...

I BICYCLED BACK TO MY APARTMENT, MARVELING AT THE DISSONANCE BETWEEN THIS APPARENTLY CAREFREE ACTIVITY AND MY NEWLY TRAGIC CIRCUMSTANCES.

AS I TOLD MY GIRLFRIEND WHAT HAD HAPPENED, I CRIED QUITE GENUINELY FOR ABOUT TWO MINUTES.

THAT WAS ALL.

JOAN DROVE HOME WITH ME AND WE ARRIVED THAT EVENING. MY LITTLE BROTHER JOHN AND I GREETED EACH OTHER WITH GHASTLY, UNCONTROLLABLE GRINS.

IT COULD BE ARGUED THAT DEATH IS INHERENTLY ABSURD, AND THAT GRINNING IS NOT NECESSARILY AN INAPPROPRIATE RESPONSE. I MEAN ABSURD IN THE SENSE OF RIDICULOUS, UNREASONABLE. ONE SECOND A PERSON IS THERE, THE NEXT THEY'RE NOT.

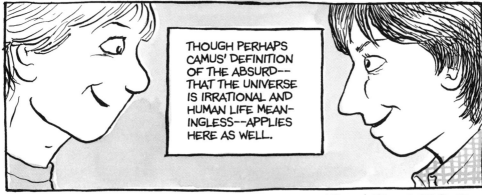

THOUGH PERHAPS CAMUS' DEFINITION OF THE ABSURD-- THAT THE UNIVERSE IS IRRATIONAL AND HUMAN LIFE MEANINGLESS--APPLIES HERE AS WELL.

IN COLLEGE, I NEEDED *THE MYTH OF SISYPHUS* FOR A CLASS. DAD OFFERED TO SEND ME HIS OLD COPY, BUT I RESISTED HIS INTERFERENCE.

S.222
INTRO. TO WESTERN PHILOSOPHY

THE MYTH OF SISYPHUS
CAMUS - The Myth of...

I WISH I COULD SAY I'D ACCEPTED HIS BOOK, THAT I STILL HAD IT, THAT HE'D UNDERLINED ONE PARTICULAR PASSAGE.

> longing for death.
> The subject of this essay is precisely this relationship between the absurd and suicide, the exact degree to which suicide is a solution to the absurd. The principle can be established that for a man who does not cheat, what he believes to be true must determine his action. Belief in the absurdity of existence must then dictate his conduct. It is legitimate to wonder, clearly and without false pathos, whether a conclusion of this importance requires forsaking as rapidly as possible an incomprehensible condition. I am

IT'S NOT THAT I THINK HE KILLED HIMSELF OUT OF EXISTENTIALIST CONVICTION. FOR ONE THING, IF HE'D READ CAREFULLY, HE WOULD HAVE GOTTEN TO CAMUS' CONCLUSION THAT SUICIDE IS ILLOGICAL.

BUT I SUSPECT MY FATHER OF BEING A HAPHAZARD SCHOLAR.

BECHDEL! PUT THAT GODDAMN BOOK DOWN. WE'RE GOING OUT.

ΦΚΨ

A SNAPSHOT OF HIM IN A FRAT BROTHER'S SPORTS CAR REMINDS ME OF CARTIER-BRESSON'S PHOTOS OF CAMUS.

MAYBE IT'S JUST THE CIGARETTE. IN EVERY PHOTO I'VE SEEN OF CAMUS, THERE'S A BUTT DANGLING FROM HIS GALLIC LIP.

BUT CAMUS' LUNGS WERE FULL OF HOLES FROM TUBERCULOSIS. WHO WAS HE TO CAST LOGICAL ASPERSIONS AT SUICIDE?

A Happy Death
a novel

TO BE FAIR, EVERY-ONE SMOKED THEN.

HE COULDN'T HAVE LASTED MUCH LONGER EVEN IF HE HADN'T DIED IN A CAR CRASH AT FORTY-SIX.

CAMUS WAS KNOWN TO HAVE SAID TO HIS FRIENDS ON VARIOUS OCCASIONS THAT DYING IN A CAR ACCIDENT WOULD BE *UNE MORT IMBÉCILE.*

IN JANUARY OF 1960, THE SPORTS CAR HE WAS RIDING IN CAROMED OFF ONE PLANE TREE AND WRAPPED AROUND ANOTHER.

PARIS
Herald Tribune
THE WRITER ALBERT CAMUS KILLED IN AUTOMOBILE ACCIDENT
NIXON MAY HURT G.O.P. PLATE

MY PARENTS WERE STILL IN EUROPE.

CAMUS ALSO SAID, IN *THE MYTH OF SISYPHUS,* THAT WE ALL LIVE AS IF WE DON'T KNOW WE'RE GOING TO DIE.

Yet one will never be sufficiently surprised that everyone lives as if no one "knew." This is because in reality there is no experience of death. Properly speaking, nothing has been experienced but what has been lived and made conscious. Here, it is barely possible to speak of the experience of others' deaths. It is a substitute, and illusion, and it never quite convinces us. That melancholy convention cannot be persuasive. The horror comes in reality from the mathematical aspect of the event. If time

BUT THEN, HE WASN'T A MORTICIAN.

I SUSPECT THAT FOR MY FATHER, DEATH WAS ALL TOO CONVINCING.

IN THE LETTERS HE SENT ME AT COLLEGE, SOMETIMES HE SEEMED THE PERFECT ABSURD HERO, SISYPHUS SHOULDERING HIS BOULDER WITH DETACHED JOY.

The weekend was of little consequense entertainmentwise. I was called at 3:30 AM for Fay Murray's death. That shot that Friday Saturday. Some highlights of my work her yellow lace bikini rose-embroidered panties. Her died red hair after three months of hospitalizatio Her hairdersser and her hairpieces. Her bitter green velvet jumpsuit with gold sequined trim and plunging neckline. Well I did my best with red lips, green eyeshadow, lots of rouge and eyebrow pencil and low and behold there lay Fay. She had lovely flawlessly smoothskin. Everyone was pleased and you would never have guessed she was <u>seventy.</u>

OTHER TIMES, HE WAS DESPAIRING.

Claude M. Bechdel Funeral Home
Telephone 717-962-2727
Beech Creek, Pennsylvania 16822

Dorothy E. Bechdel

Bruce A. Bechdel

Sunday 9-24-77

Dear Al-

I'm at fun home, tending local tragedy. Beautiful girl, 38, wrapped her car around one of those big trees in the Rupert's front yard. Worked eighteen hours yesterday, now I'm here fighting off the ghouls — it's bad for my blood pressure.

I DON'T HAVE ANY LETTERS ABOUT THE SUICIDES HE DEALT WITH, LIKE THE LOCAL DOCTOR WHO SHOT HIMSELF A FEW MONTHS BEFORE DAD'S OWN DEATH.

BUT YOU WOULD THINK THAT LONG NIGHTS EMPLOYED IN THIS SCUTWORK OF THE FLESH WOULD MAKE ANY-ONE RECONSIDER THE LOGIC OF NOT POSTPONING THE INEVITABLE.

YOU WOULD ALSO THINK THAT A CHILDHOOD SPENT IN SUCH CLOSE PROXIMITY TO THE WORKADAY INCIDENTALS OF DEATH WOULD BE GOOD PREPARATION.

THAT WHEN SOMEONE YOU KNEW ACTUALLY DIED, MAYBE YOU'D GET TO SKIP A PHASE OR TWO OF THE GRIEVING PROCESS--"DENIAL" AND "ANGER," FOR EXAMPLE--

BUT IN FACT, ALL THE YEARS SPENT VISITING GRAVEDIGGERS, JOKING WITH BURIAL-VAULT SALESMEN, AND TEASING MY BROTHERS WITH CRUSHED VIALS OF SMELLING SALTS ONLY MADE MY OWN FATHER'S DEATH MORE INCOMPREHENSIBLE.

WHO EMBALMS THE UNDERTAKER WHEN HE DIES?

IT WAS LIKE RUSSELL'S PARADOX...

...THE FAMOUS CONUNDRUM OF THE CLEAN-SHAVEN BARBER WHOSE SIGN READS, "I SHAVE ALL THOSE MEN, AND ONLY THOSE MEN, WHO DO NOT SHAVE THEMSELVES."

THE BARBER, EQUALLY UNABLE TO SHAVE HIMSELF, AND TO NOT SHAVE HIMSELF, IS IMPOSSIBLE.

YET SOMEHOW, THERE HE IS.

MY FATHER COULD HAVE USED A BARBER. HIS FACE WAS ROUGH AND DRY, SCRAPED CLEAN WITH NO HELP FROM THE EXPENSIVE LOTIONS AND AFTERSHAVES ON THE SILVER TRAY IN HIS BATHROOM AT HOME.

HIS WIRY HAIR, WHICH HE HAD DAILY TAKEN GREAT PAINS TO STYLE, WAS BRUSHED STRAIGHT UP ON END AND REVEALED A SURPRISINGLY RECEDED HAIRLINE.

I WASN'T EVEN SURE IT WAS HIM UNTIL I FOUND THE TINY BLUE TATTOO ON HIS KNUCKLE WHERE HE'D ONCE BEEN ACCIDENTALLY STABBED WITH A PENCIL.

DRY-EYED AND SHEEPISH, MY BROTHERS AND I LOOKED FOR AS LONG AS WE SENSED IT WAS APPROPRIATE.

IF ONLY THEY MADE SMELLING SALTS TO INDUCE GRIEF-STRICKEN SWOONS, RATHER THAN SNAP YOU OUT OF THEM.

THE SOLE EMOTION I COULD MUSTER WAS IRRITATION, WHEN THE PINCH-FUNERAL DIRECTOR LAID HIS HAND ON MY ARM CONSOLINGLY.

I SHOOK IT OFF WITH A VIOLENCE THAT WAS, IN FACT, RATHER CONSOLING.

THIS SAME IRRITATION WOULD OVERTAKE ME FOR YEARS AFTERWARD WHEN I VISITED DAD'S GRAVE.

ON ONE OCCASION I FOUND IT DESECRATED WITH A CHEESY FLAG, PLACED THERE BY SOME WELL-MEANING ARMED SERVICES ORGANIZATION.

I JAVELINED THIS, UGLY BRASS HOLDER AND ALL, INTO THE CORNFIELD THAT IMMEDIATELY ADJOINS HIS PLOT AT THE EDGE OF THE CEMETERY.

AGAIN, THERE WAS SOME FLEETING CONSOLATION IN THE SHEER VIOLENCE OF MY GESTURE.

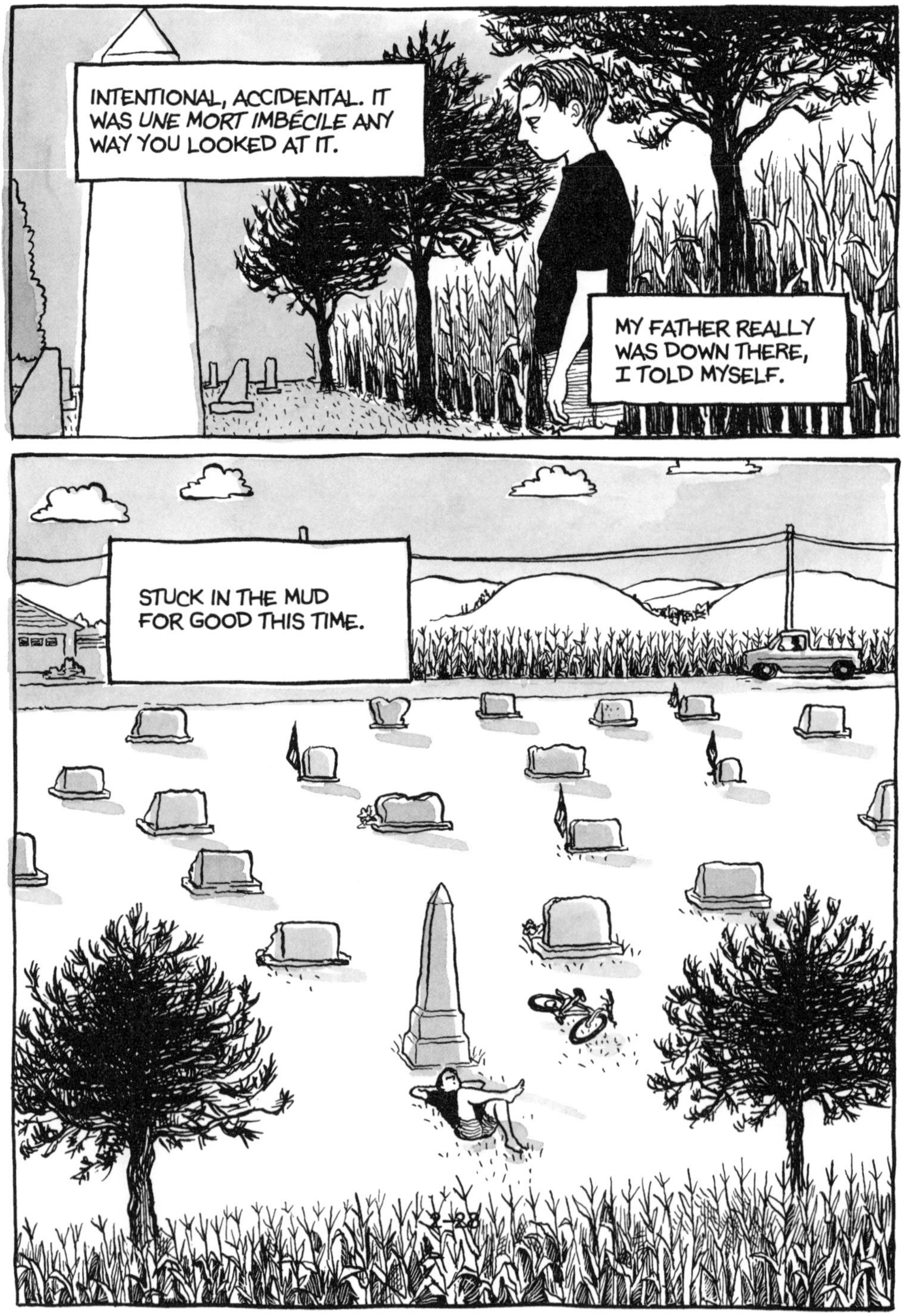
INTENTIONAL, ACCIDENTAL. IT WAS *UNE MORT IMBÉCILE* ANY WAY YOU LOOKED AT IT.
MY FATHER REALLY WAS DOWN THERE, I TOLD MYSELF.
STUCK IN THE MUD FOR GOOD THIS TIME.

CHAPTER 3

THAT OLD CATASTROPHE

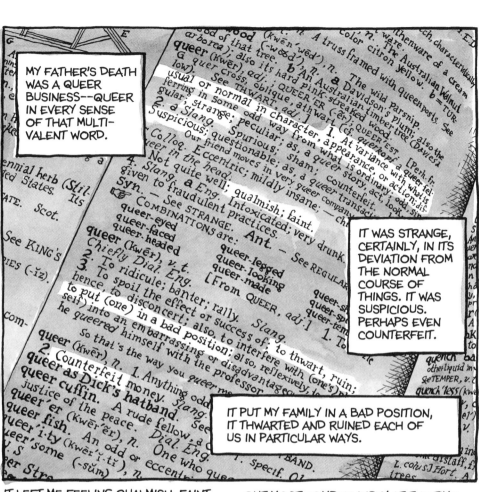

MY FATHER'S DEATH WAS A QUEER BUSINESS--QUEER IN EVERY SENSE OF THAT MULTI-VALENT WORD.

IT WAS STRANGE, CERTAINLY, IN ITS DEVIATION FROM THE NORMAL COURSE OF THINGS. IT WAS SUSPICIOUS. PERHAPS EVEN COUNTERFEIT.

IT PUT MY FAMILY IN A BAD POSITION, IT THWARTED AND RUINED EACH OF US IN PARTICULAR WAYS.

IT LEFT ME FEELING QUALMISH, FAINT, AND, ON OCCASION, DRUNK.

BUT MOST COMPELLINGLY AT THE TIME, HIS DEATH WAS BOUND UP FOR ME WITH THE ONE DEFINITION CONSPICUOUSLY MISSING FROM OUR MAMMOTH WEBSTER'S.

ONLY FOUR MONTHS EARLIER, I HAD MADE AN ANNOUNCEMENT TO MY PARENTS.

MY HOMOSEXUALITY REMAINED AT THAT POINT PURELY THEORETICAL, AN UNTESTED HYPOTHESIS.

BUT IT WAS A HYPOTHESIS SO THOROUGH AND CONVINCING THAT I SAW NO REASON NOT TO SHARE IT IMMEDIATELY.

THE NEWS WAS NOT RECEIVED AS WELL AS I HAD HOPED. THERE WAS AN EXCHANGE OF DIFFICULT LETTERS WITH MY MOTHER.

THEN A PHONE CALL IN WHICH SHE DEALT A STAGGERING BLOW.

I'D BEEN UPSTAGED, DEMOTED FROM PROTAGONIST IN MY OWN DRAMA TO COMIC RELIEF IN MY PARENTS' TRAGEDY.

I HAD IMAGINED MY CONFESSION AS AN EMANCIPATION FROM MY PARENTS, BUT INSTEAD I WAS PULLED BACK INTO THEIR ORBIT.

AND WITH MY FATHER'S DEATH FOLLOWING SO HARD ON THE HEELS OF THIS DOLEFUL COMING-OUT PARTY, I COULD NOT HELP BUT ASSUME A CAUSE-AND-EFFECT RELATIONSHIP.

IF I HAD NOT FELT COMPELLED TO SHARE MY LITTLE SEXUAL DISCOVERY, PERHAPS THE SEMI WOULD HAVE PASSED WITHOUT INCIDENT FOUR MONTHS LATER.

(YES, IT REALLY WAS A SUNBEAM BREAD TRUCK.)

WHY HAD I TOLD THEM? I HADN'T EVEN HAD SEX WITH ANYONE YET. CONVERSELY, MY FATHER HAD BEEN HAVING SEX WITH MEN FOR YEARS AND NOT TELLING ANYONE.

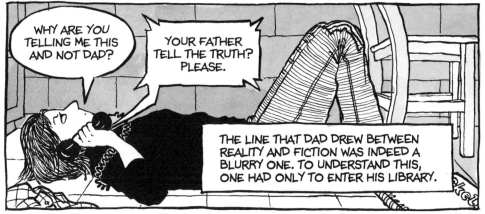

WHY ARE YOU TELLING ME THIS AND NOT DAD?

YOUR FATHER TELL THE TRUTH? PLEASE.

THE LINE THAT DAD DREW BETWEEN REALITY AND FICTION WAS INDEED A BLURRY ONE. TO UNDERSTAND THIS, ONE HAD ONLY TO ENTER HIS LIBRARY.

FOR ANYONE BUT THE LANDED GENTRY TO REFER TO A ROOM IN THEIR HOUSE AS "THE LIBRARY" MIGHT SEEM AFFECTED. BUT THERE REALLY WAS NO OTHER WORD FOR IT.

FLOCKED

GILT

VELVET

DON QUIXOTE

MEPHI-STOPHELES

AND IF MY FATHER LIKED TO IMAGINE HIMSELF AS A NINETEENTH-CENTURY ARISTOCRAT OVERSEEING HIS ESTATE FROM BEHIND THE LEATHER-TOPPED MAHOGANY AND BRASS SECOND-EMPIRE DESK...

...DID THAT REQUIRE SUCH A LEAP OF THE IMAGINATION? PERHAPS AFFECTATION CAN BE SO THOROUGHGOING, SO AUTHENTIC IN ITS DETAILS, THAT IT STOPS BEING PRETENSE...

...AND BECOMES, FOR ALL PRACTICAL PURPOSES, REAL.

THE LIBRARY WAS A FANTASY, BUT A FULLY OPERATIONAL ONE.

WHERE'S IRKUTSK?

LOOK IN THE ATLAS.

WHERE'S THE ATLAS?

IN THE CANTERBURY ATLAS RACK.

VISITORS ALWAYS ASKED THE SAME QUESTION ABOUT THE MASSIVE WALNUT BOOKCASE.

SO, BRUCE, HAVE YOU READ ALL THOSE?

NOT YET.

PART OF DAD'S COUNTRY SQUIRE ROUTINE INVOLVED EDIFYING THE VILLAGERS--HIS MORE PROMISING HIGH SCHOOL STUDENTS.

THIS WAS GREAT. WHAT'S NEXT?

THE PROMISE WAS VERY LIKELY SEXUAL IN SOME CASES, BUT WHATEVER ELSE MIGHT HAVE BEEN GOING ON, BOOKS WERE BEING READ.

DAD WAS PASSIONATE ABOUT MANY WRITERS, BUT HE HAD A PARTICULAR REVERENCE FOR FITZGERALD.

MY MOTHER HAD SENT HIM A BIOGRAPHY OF FITZGERALD BEFORE THEY MARRIED, WHEN DAD WAS IN THE ARMY.

HE'D BEEN DRAFTED AFTER DROPPING OUT OF HIS GRADUATE ENGLISH PROGRAM, OVERWHELMED WITH THE WORKLOAD.

REFERENCES TO THE BIOGRAPHY CREPT INTO HIS LETTERS TO HER.

THE TALES OF SCOTT AND ZELDA'S DRUNKEN, OUTRAGEOUS BEHAVIOR CAPTIVATED HIM.

IT COULD NOT HAVE ESCAPED MY FATHER'S NOTICE THAT DURING SCOTT'S OWN STINT IN THE ARMY HE WROTE HIS FIRST NOVEL AND BEGAN COURTING ZELDA.

DAD'S LETTERS TO MOM, WHICH HAD NOT BEEN PARTICULARLY DEMONSTRATIVE UP TO THIS POINT, BEGAN TO GROW LUSH WITH FITZGERALDESQUE SENTIMENT.

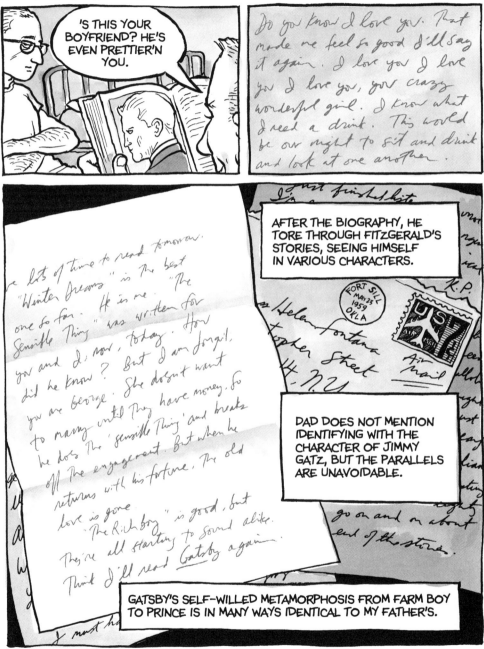

LIKE GATSBY, MY FATHER FUELED THIS TRANSFORMATION WITH "THE COLOSSAL VITALITY OF HIS ILLUSION." UNLIKE GATSBY, HE DID IT ON A SCHOOLTEACHER'S SALARY.

IT'S THE GREAT AMERICAN NOVEL.

THE GREAT GATSBY

EVEN SO, HIS NOBLESSE OBLIGE WAS ENTIRELY GENUINE.

MY FATHER EVEN LOOKED LIKE GATSBY, OR AT ANY RATE, LIKE ROBERT REDFORD IN THE 1974 MOVIE.

MY PARENTS TOOK US TO SEE THIS THE MOMENT IT OPENED.

PERHAPS IT SEEMS LIKE A COLOSSAL ILLUSION ON MY PART TO COMPARE MY FATHER TO ROBERT REDFORD.

(ANNUAL SCHOOL PORTRAIT)

BUT HE WAS MORE ATTRAC-TIVE THAN THE PHOTO-GRAPHIC RECORD REVEALS.

ZELDA FITZGERALD ALSO HAD A FLUID CHARM, IT WAS SAID, WHICH ELUDED THE STILL CAMERA.

I THINK WHAT WAS SO ALLURING TO MY FATHER ABOUT FITZGERALD'S STORIES WAS THEIR INEXTRICABILITY FROM FITZGERALD'S LIFE.

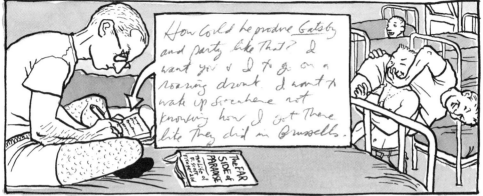

SUCH A SUSPENSION OF THE IMAGINARY IN THE REAL WAS, AFTER ALL, MY FATHER'S STOCK IN TRADE.

IF MY FATHER WAS A FITZGERALD CHARACTER, MY MOTHER STEPPED RIGHT OUT OF HENRY JAMES—A VIGOROUS AMERICAN IDEALIST ENSNARED BY DEGENERATE CONTINENTAL FORCES.

WANNA COME ALONG?

IN FACT, IN COLLEGE SHE PLAYED THE LEAD IN *THE HEIRESS*, WHICH IS BASED ON JAMES'S NOVEL *WASHINGTON SQUARE*.

A PLAIN, DULL, BUT WEALTHY YOUNG WOMAN FALLS IN LOVE WITH THE SMOOTH-TALKING FORTUNE HUNTER, MORRIS TOWNSEND.

I AM NOT VERY GOOD AT THIS KIND OF CONVERSATION.

NEITHER AM I. I AM AFRAID THAT IS OUR TROUBLE—I AM NOT A GLIB MAN, MISS SLOPER.

IN A TWIST ON THE USUAL HETEROSEXUAL TROPE...

...CATHERINE IS THE LOVER, AND MORRIS, THE BELOVED.

OH, FATHER, DON'T YOU THINK HE'S THE MOST BEAUTIFUL MAN YOU'VE EVER SEEN?

HE IS VERY GOOD-LOOKING.

I BOUGHT YOU A SET OF BUTTONS... RUBIES AND PEARLS.

MY DEAR, DEAR GIRL.

I EMPLOY THESE ALLUSIONS TO JAMES AND FITZGERALD NOT ONLY AS DESCRIPTIVE DEVICES, BUT BECAUSE MY PARENTS ARE MOST REAL TO ME IN FICTIONAL TERMS.

AND PERHAPS MY COOL AESTHETIC DISTANCE ITSELF DOES MORE TO CONVEY THE ARCTIC CLIMATE OF OUR FAMILY THAN ANY PARTICULAR LITERARY COMPARISON.

MEATBALLS

MY PARENTS SEEMED ALMOST EMBARRASSED BY THE FACT OF THEIR MARRIAGE. THERE WAS NO STORY, FOR EXAMPLE, OF HOW THEY MET.

HOW DID YOU MEET DAD?

RING!

THEY DID NOT USE TERMS OF ENDEAR-MENT. THE DAYS OF MY FATHER'S SENTI-MENTAL LETTERS WERE LONG GONE.

IN FACT, HE PERVERSELY AVOIDED ADDRESSING MY MOTHER WITH EVEN HER GIVEN NAME.

I WITNESSED ONLY TWO GESTURES OF AFFECTION BETWEEN THEM. ONCE MY FATHER GAVE MY MOTHER A CHASTE PECK BEFORE LEAVING ON A WEEKEND TRIP.

AND ONE TIME MY MOTHER PUT HER HAND ON HIS BACK AS WE WERE WATCHING TV.

THESE STRAY RENTS IN THE OTHERWISE SEAMLESS FABRIC OF THEIR ANTAGONISM...

...WERE VERY NEARLY AS UNNERVING AS THE ANTAGONISM ITSELF.

MY PARENTS MET, I EVENTUALLY EXTRACTED FROM MY MOTHER, IN A PERFORMANCE OF *THE TAMING OF THE SHREW.*

WHAT WAS THAT?

SOUNDS LIKE HE KNOCKED A STACK OF BOOKS OFF THE DESK.

CRASH!

...AND TO CONCLUDE, WE HAVE 'GREED SO WELL TOGETHER THAT UPON SUNDAY IS THE WEDDING DAY!

IT WAS A COLLEGE PRODUCTION. MY FATHER HAD A BIT PART AS ONE OF THE MEN. MOM PLAYED THE LEAD.

I'LL SEE THEE HANG'D ON SUNDAY FIRST.

IT'S A TROUBLING PLAY, OF COURSE. THE WILLFUL KATHERINE'S SPIRIT IS BROKEN BY THE MERCENARY, DOMINEERING PETRUCHIO.

I SAY IT IS THE MOON THAT SHINES SO BRIGHTLY.

I **KNOW** IT IS THE **SUN** THAT SHINES SO BRIGHTLY.

I SPECULATE ON WHAT ATTRACTED MY FATHER MORE--THE ROLE, THE ACTRESS, OR MY MOTHER HERSELF.

SAY AS HE SAYS, OR WE SHALL NEVER GO!

EVEN IN THOSE PREFEMINIST DAYS, MY PARENTS MUST HAVE FOUND THIS RELATION-
SHIP MODEL TO BE PROBLEMATIC.

THEY WOULD PROBABLY HAVE BEEN APPALLED AT THE SUGGESTION THAT THEIR OWN
MARRIAGE WOULD PLAY OUT IN A SIMILAR WAY.

IF *THE TAMING
OF THE SHREW*
WAS A
HARBINGER OF
MY PARENTS'
LATER MARRIAGE,
HENRY JAMES'S
*THE PORTRAIT
OF A LADY*
RUNS MORE
THAN A LITTLE
PARALLEL TO
THEIR EARLY
DAYS
TOGETHER.

70

ISABEL ARCHER, THE HEROINE, LEAVES AMERICA FOR EUROPE. SHE'S FILLED WITH HEADY NOTIONS ABOUT LIVING HER LIFE FREE FROM PROVINCIAL CONVENTION AND CONSTRAINT.

ISABEL TURNS DOWN A NUMBER OF WORTHY SUITORS, BUT PERVERSELY ACCEPTS GILBERT OSMOND, A CULTURED, DISSIPATED, AND PENNILESS EUROPEAN ART COLLECTOR.

(MOM'S PASSPORT FROM HER TRIP TO GERMANY TO MARRY MY FATHER)

MY PARENTS MADE A TRIP TO PARIS SOON AFTER THEIR WEDDING, TO VISIT AN ARMY FRIEND OF MY FATHER'S.

LATER, MY MOTHER WOULD LEARN THAT DAD AND HIS FRIEND HAD BEEN LOVERS.

HE'S A WRITER. YOU'LL LOVE HIM.

THEY HAD A TERRIBLE FIGHT IN THE CAR.

CAN'T YOU READ A SIMPLE FUCKING MAP?!

MUCH LIKE ISABEL ARCHER LEARNS THAT GILBERT HAD BEEN HAVING AN AFFAIR ALL ALONG WITH THE WOMAN WHO INTRODUCED THEM.

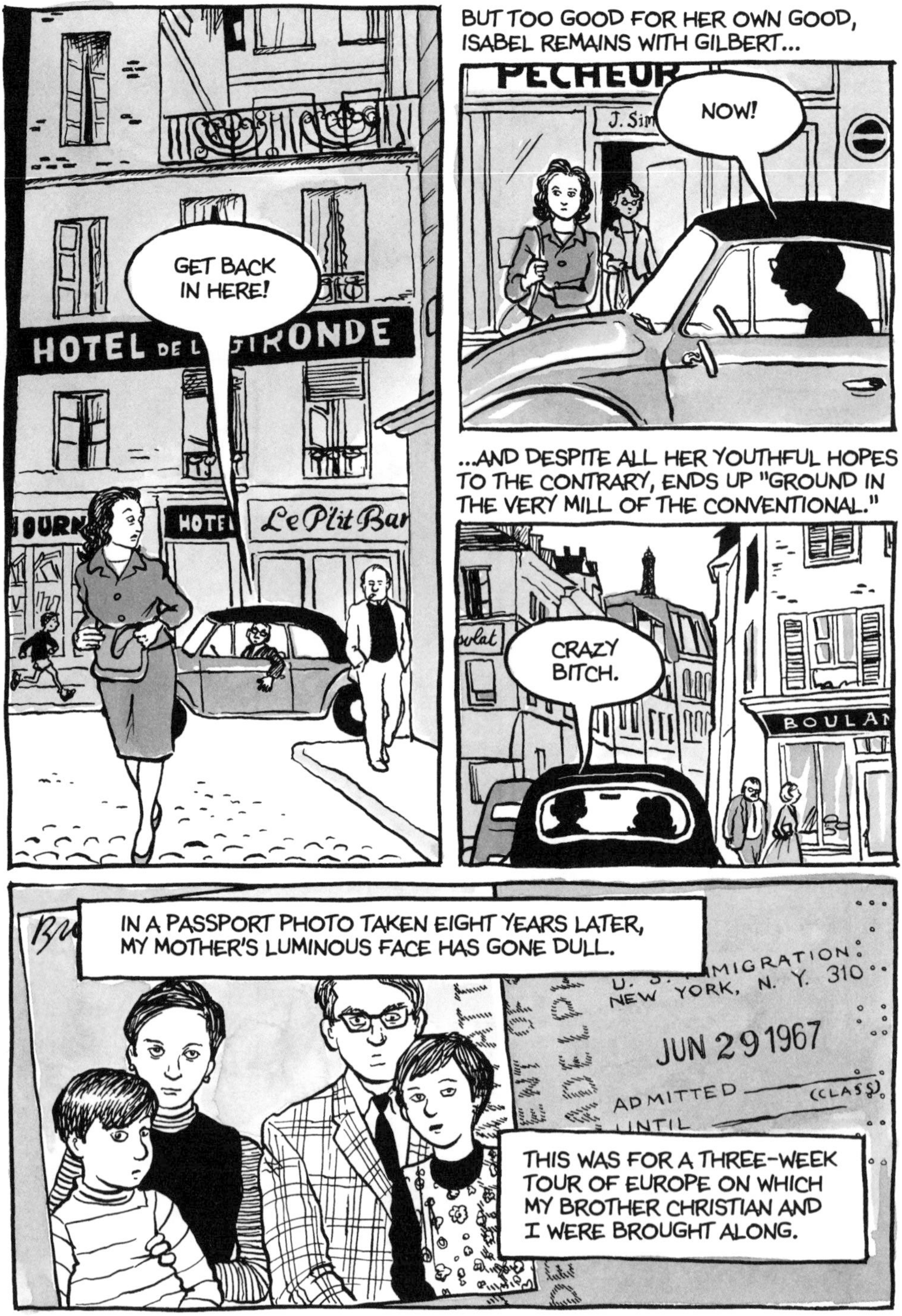
GET BACK IN HERE!
BUT TOO GOOD FOR HER OWN GOOD, ISABEL REMAINS WITH GILBERT...
NOW!
...AND DESPITE ALL HER YOUTHFUL HOPES TO THE CONTRARY, ENDS UP "GROUND IN THE VERY MILL OF THE CONVENTIONAL."
CRAZY BITCH.
IN A PASSPORT PHOTO TAKEN EIGHT YEARS LATER, MY MOTHER'S LUMINOUS FACE HAS GONE DULL.
NEW YORK, N. Y. 310
JUN 29 1967
ADMITTED
(CLASS)
THIS WAS FOR A THREE-WEEK TOUR OF EUROPE ON WHICH MY BROTHER CHRISTIAN AND I WERE BROUGHT ALONG.

IT WAS A THRILLING TRIP. IN SWITZER-
LAND I TALKED MY PARENTS INTO
BUYING ME HIKING BOOTS.

IN CANNES, I ARGUED COMPELLINGLY
FOR THE RIGHT TO EXCHANGE MY TANK
SUIT FOR A PAIR OF SHORTS.

SUCH FREEDOM FROM CONVENTION WAS INTOXICATING. BUT WHILE OUR TRAVELS
WIDENED MY SCOPE, I SUSPECT MY PARENTS FELT THEIR OWN DWINDLING.

PERHAPS THIS WAS WHEN I CEMENTED THE UNSPOKEN COMPACT WITH THEM THAT I
WOULD NEVER GET MARRIED, THAT I WOULD CARRY ON TO LIVE THE ARTIST'S LIFE
THEY HAD EACH ABDICATED.

73

THAT IS IN FACT WHAT CAME TO PASS, BUT NOT IN THE WAY ANY OF US HAD EXPECTED.

MY REALIZATION AT NINETEEN THAT I WAS A LESBIAN CAME ABOUT IN A MANNER CONSISTENT WITH MY BOOKISH UPBRINGING.

A REVELATION NOT OF THE FLESH, BUT OF THE MIND.

I'D BEEN HAVING QUALMS SINCE I WAS THIRTEEN...

...WHEN I FIRST LEARNED THE WORD DUE TO ITS ALARMING PROMINENCE IN MY DICTIONARY.

lesbian

¹les·bi·an \'lez-bē-ən\ adj, often cap 1 : of or relati
2 [fr. the reputed homosexual band associated wit
Lesbos] : of or relating to homosexuality between fer
²lesbian n, often cap : a female homosexual
les·bi·an·ism \-ə-,niz-əm\ n ; female homosexuality
lèse maj·es·ty or lèse ma·jes·té \'lēz-'maj-ə-stē
majesté fr. L læsa majestas, lit. injured majesty] 1
committed against a sovereign power b : an offense

BUT NOW ANOTHER BOOK--A BOOK ABOUT PEOPLE WHO HAD COMPLETELY CAST ASIDE THEIR OWN QUALMS--ELABORATED ON THAT DEFINITION.

Elsa

NANCY: Do you mind saying how old you are?

ELSA: I'm 77. I was born in December 1898.

N: How long have you been a lesbian?

E: I never understood what that means, because as far as I'm concerned I was born that way. I never had that crossing-over crisis that people talk about these days - the feeling that you have to have some kind of an indoctri... or trauma, or a coming-out ritual. I just knew th... different in many ways from what was... was always interested in why I was...
what it is all about in...

THAT FIRST VOLUME LED QUICKLY TO OTHERS.

A FEW DAYS LATER I SCREWED UP MY COURAGE AND BOUGHT ONE.

THIS BOOK REFERRED TO OTHER BOOKS, WHICH I SOUGHT OUT IN THE LIBRARY.

ONE DAY IT OCCURRED TO ME THAT I COULD ACTUALLY LOOK UP *HOMOSEXUALITY* IN THE CARD CATALOG.

I FOUND A FOUR-FOOT TROVE IN THE STACKS WHICH I QUICKLY RAVISHED.

AND SOON I WAS TROLLING EVEN THE PUBLIC LIBRARY, HEEDLESS OF THE RISKS.

75

MY RESEARCHES WERE STIMULATING BUT SOLITARY.

GENERAL CHART of THE SKY

IT BECAME CLEAR I WAS GOING TO HAVE TO LEAVE THIS ACADEMIC PLANE AND ENTER THE HUMAN FRAY.

I WENT TO A MEETING OF SOMETHING CALLED THE "GAY UNION," WHICH I OBSERVED IN PETRIFIED SILENCE.

BUT MY MERE PRESENCE, I FELT, HAD AMOUNTED TO A PUBLIC DECLARATION. I LEFT EXHILARATED.

IT WAS IN THAT TREMULOUS STATE THAT I DETERMINED TO TELL MY PARENTS. KEEPING IT FROM THEM HAD STARTED TO SEEM LUDICROUS ANYWAY.

WHAT ARE YOU READING? ANYTHING GOOD?

UH...NOT REALLY.

76

I DID IT VIA LETTER--A REMOTE MEDIUM, BUT AS I HAVE EXPLAINED, WE WERE THAT SORT OF FAMILY.

MY FATHER CALLED AFTER RECEIVING IT. HE SEEMED STRANGELY PLEASED TO THINK I WAS HAVING SOME KIND OF ORGY.

EVERYONE SHOULD EXPERIMENT. IT'S HEALTHY.

MOM WOULDN'T COME TO THE PHONE.

UHH...SHE'S WATCHING SOMETHING ON TV. SHE WAS PRETTY UPSET.

BUT HER RETURN EPISTLE ARRIVED A WEEK AND A HALF LATER.

AS DISAPPROVAL GOES, I SUPPOSE IT WAS RATHER MILD.

STILL, I WAS DEVASTATED.

77

HER P.S. INSTRUCTED ME TO DESTROY THE LETTER.

IN AN ATTEMPT TO SALVE THE WOUND, I BOUGHT MYSELF A PRESENT.

A SYMBOL OF SELF-RELIANCE? AT ANY RATE, IT SEEMED LIKE SOMETHING A LESBIAN WOULD HAVE.

OPENING IT BACK IN MY ROOM, I ACCIDENTALLY CUT MY FINGER.

I SMEARED THE BLOOD INTO MY JOURNAL, PLEASED BY THE OPPORTUNITY TO TRANSMIT MY ANGUISH TO THE PAGE SO LITERALLY.

I RESPONDED TO MY MOTHER'S LETTER POINT BY POINT.

And regarding your third paragraph, no, I have no idea what you're talking about. What catastrophe?

Smith-Corona

SHE FILLED ME IN A FEW DAYS LATER.

DAD? WITH OTHER MEN?

AND BOYS. ONE TIME HE ALMOST GOT CAUGHT. AND THEN THERE WAS THE THING WITH ROY.

THIS ABRUPT AND WHOLESALE REVISION OF MY HISTORY--A HISTORY WHICH, I MIGHT ADD, HAD ALREADY BEEN REVISED ONCE IN THE PRECEDING MONTHS--LEFT ME STUPEFIED.

ROY, OUR BABY-SITTER?!

BUT NOT QUITE STUPEFIED ENOUGH--A CONDITION WHICH I REMEDIED UPON HANGING UP THE PHONE.

PLASTIC TUBING AVAILABLE AT ANY HARDWARE STORE

SIMPLE MASON JAR

SOON, HOWEVER, I DISCOVERED AN EVEN MORE POTENT ANESTHETIC.

MARCH ON HINGTON for ESBIAN & y RIGHTS CT. 14

...AND WE NEED PEOPLE TO PUT UP FLYERS ABOUT OUR CONFERENCE.

THE NOTION THAT MY SORDID PERSONAL LIFE HAD SOME SORT OF LARGER IMPORT WAS STRANGE, BUT SEDUCTIVE.

AND BY MIDTERM I HAD BEEN SEDUCED COMPLETELY.

FEMINISM IS THE THEORY. LESBIANISM IS THE PRACTICE.

GAY DANCE

GRAIN ALCOHOL

JOAN WAS A POET AND A "MATRIARCHIST." I SPENT VERY LITTLE OF THE REMAINING SEMESTER OUTSIDE HER BED.

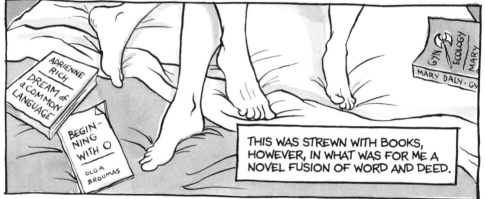

ADRIENNE RICH
DREAM of a COMMON LANGUAGE

BEGINNING WITH O
OLGA BROUMAS

GYN/ECOLOGY · MARY
MARY DALY · GY

THIS WAS STREWN WITH BOOKS, HOWEVER, IN WHAT WAS FOR ME A NOVEL FUSION OF WORD AND DEED.

I LOST MY BEARINGS. THE DICTIONARY HAD BECOME EROTIC.

OS-. MOUTH. ORAL, OSCILLATE, OSCULATE, ORIFICE...

INDEX OF INDO-EUROPEAN ROOTS

OH.

SOME OF OUR FAVORITE CHILDHOOD STORIES WERE REVEALED AS PROPAGANDA...

GOD. CHRISTOPHER ROBIN'S A TOTAL IMPERIALIST!

The WORLD of POOH

...OTHERS AS PORNOGRAPHY. IN THE HARSH LIGHT OF MY DAWNING FEMINISM, EVERYTHING LOOKED DIFFERENT.

...THE WALLS WERE WET AND STICKY, AND PEACH JUICE WAS DRIPPING FROM THE CEILING. JAMES OPENED HIS MOUTH AND CAUGHT SOME OF IT ON HIS TONGUE.

THIS ENTWINED POLITICAL AND SEXUAL AWAKENING WAS A WELCOME DISTRACTION.

...IT TASTED DELICIOUS.

RING!

THE NEWS FROM HOME WAS INCREASINGLY UNSETTLING.

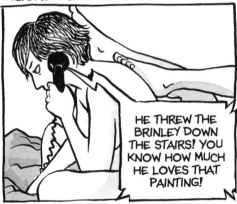

HE THREW THE BRINLEY DOWN THE STAIRS! YOU KNOW HOW MUCH HE LOVES THAT PAINTING!

SOON AFTER JOAN AND I HAD MOVED IN TOGETHER FOR THE SUMMER, I GOT MOM'S CALL ABOUT THE DIVORCE.

I'VE HAD IT.

AND TWO WEEKS AFTER THAT, THE CALL ABOUT THE ACCIDENT.

IS HE DEAD?

OVER THE YEARS, MY MOTHER HAS GIVEN AWAY OR SOLD MOST OF DAD'S LIBRARY.

JOAN, YOU'VE BEEN SO HELPFUL WITH EVERYTHING...

SHE BEGAN IMMEDIATELY AFTER THE FUNERAL, BESTOWING A BOOK ON JOAN.

LATER, JOAN WROTE A POEM ABOUT IT.

You're sitting in the library
feet up on his desk.

Your mother comes in
her face warm and white
floating gingerly over her
bathrobe.

She tells me to choose a book.

Cloth-bound, grey and turquoise
heavy in my hand as a turtle shell
filled with mud.

ARE YOU SURE?

YES. AND DON'T JUST PICK A CHEAP PAPERBACK. TAKE SOMETHING GOOD.

OUT OF THE HUNDREDS OF BOOKS ON THE SHELVES, I DON'T THINK SHE COULD HAVE MADE A BETTER CHOICE.

HOW ABOUT THIS?

OH, I LOVE WALLACE STEVENS. DO YOU KNOW "SUNDAY MORNING"? IT'S MY FAVORITE POEM.

"COMPLACENCIES OF THE PEIGNOIR, AND LATE COFFEE AND ORANGES IN A SUNNY CHAIR..."

IT'S ABOUT THE CRUCIFIXION.

"...AND THE GREEN FREEDOM OF A COCKATOO UPON A RUG MINGLE TO DISSIPATE THE HOLY HUSH OF ANCIENT SACRIFICE."

(HONEST TO GOD, WE HAD A PAINTING OF A COCKATOO IN THE LIBRARY.)

IN MANY WAYS MY MOTHER'S CATHOLICISM WAS MORE FORM THAN CONTENT...

...BUT SACRIFICE WAS A PRINCIPLE THAT SHE GRASPED INSTINCTIVELY.

"SHE DREAMS A LITTLE AND SHE FEELS THE DARK ENCROACHMENT OF THAT OLD CATASTROPHE AS A CALM DARKENS AMONG WATER-LIGHTS."

HELEN, KEEP THIS. I'LL PICK SOMETHING ELSE.

NO, NO. TAKE IT.

PERHAPS SHE ALSO LIKED THE POEM BECAUSE ITS JUXTAPOSITION OF CATASTROPHE WITH A PLUSH DOMESTIC INTERIOR IS LIFE WITH MY FATHER IN A NUTSHELL.

DAD'S DEATH WAS NOT A NEW CATASTROPHE BUT AN OLD ONE THAT HAD BEEN UNFOLDING VERY SLOWLY FOR A LONG TIME.

CAUSALITY IMPLIES CONNECTION, CONTACT OF SOME KIND. AND HOWEVER CONVINCING THEY MIGHT BE, YOU CAN'T LAY HANDS ON A FICTIONAL CHARACTER.

THE IDEA THAT I CAUSED HIS DEATH BY TELLING MY PARENTS I WAS A LESBIAN IS PERHAPS ILLOGICAL.

DAD?

THERE'S A SCENE IN *THE GREAT GATSBY* WHERE A DRUNKEN PARTY GUEST IS CARRIED AWAY BY THE DISCOVERY THAT THE VOLUMES IN GATSBY'S LIBRARY ARE NOT CARD-BOARD FAKES.

"WHAT THOROUGHNESS, WHAT REALISM!" HE EXCLAIMS. "KNEW WHEN TO STOP, TOO. DIDN'T CUT THE PAGES!"

WHAT.

MY FATHER'S BOOKS--THE HARDBOUND ONES WITH THEIR RAGGED DUST JACKETS, THE PAPERBACKS WITH THEIR CREASED SPINES--HAD CLEARLY BEEN READ.

BUT IN A WAY GATSBY'S PRISTINE BOOKS AND MY FATHER'S WORN ONES SIGNIFY THE SAME THING--THE PREFERENCE OF A FICTION TO REALITY.

IF FITZGERALD'S OWN LIFE HADN'T TURNED FROM FAIRY TALE TO TRAGEDY, WOULD HIS STORIES OF DISENCHANTMENT HAVE RESONATED SO DEEPLY WITH MY FATHER?

Zelda, Scott and Scottie on the Riviera, 1924

I NEED A CHECK.

GATSBY IN THE POOL. ZELDA IN THE ASYLUM. SCOTT IN HOLLYWOOD, AN ALCOHOLIC, DYING OF A HEART ATTACK AT FORTY-FOUR.

WHAT FOR?

MY FATHER WAS FORTY-FOUR WHEN HE DIED, TOO.

STRUCK BY THE COINCIDENCE, I COUNTED OUT THEIR LIFESPANS. THE SAME NUMBER OF MONTHS, THE SAME NUMBER OF WEEKS...BUT FITZGERALD LIVED THREE DAYS LONGER.

SOME NEW MAD BOOKS. THEY COST $3.70.

WRITE IT OUT AND I'LL SIGN IT.

FOR A WILD MOMENT I ENTERTAINED THE IDEA THAT MY FATHER HAD TIMED HIS DEATH WITH THIS IN MIND, AS SOME SORT OF DERANGED TRIBUTE.

BUT THAT WOULD ONLY CONFIRM THAT HIS DEATH WAS NOT MY FAULT. THAT, IN FACT, IT HAD NOTHING TO DO WITH ME AT ALL.

AND I'M RELUCTANT TO LET GO OF THAT LAST, TENUOUS BOND.

CHAPTER 4

IN THE SHADOW
OF YOUNG GIRLS
IN FLOWER

I HAVE SUGGESTED THAT MY FATHER KILLED HIMSELF, BUT IT'S JUST AS ACCURATE TO SAY THAT HE DIED GARDENING.

HE'D BEEN CLEARING BRUSH FROM THE YARD OF AN OLD FARMHOUSE HE WAS PLANNING TO RESTORE...

...AND HAD JUST CROSSED ROUTE 150 TO TOSS AN ARMLOAD OVER THE BANK.

THE TRUCK DRIVER DESCRIBED MY FATHER AS JUMPING BACKWARD INTO THE ROAD "AS IF HE SAW A SNAKE."

AND WHO KNOWS. PERHAPS HE DID.

OF ALL HIS DOMESTIC INCLINATIONS, MY FATHER'S DECIDED BENT FOR GARDENING WAS THE MOST REDOLENT TO ME OF THAT OTHER, MORE DEEPLY DISTURBING BENT.

I HATE FLOWERS.

SPRINKLE IN A LITTLE FERTILIZER, THEN PUT THE BULB IN POINTY SIDE UP.

WHAT KIND OF MAN BUT A SISSY COULD POSSIBLY LOVE FLOWERS THIS ARDENTLY?

OUR HOME WAS AN EFFLORESCENCE OF BULBS, BUDS, AND BLOOMS, FLOWERS WILD AND CULTIVATED, NATIVE AND IMPORTED, FLOWERING VINES AND TREES...

...SILK FLOWERS, GLASS FLOWERS, NEEDLEPOINT FLOWERS, FLOWER PAINTINGS AND, WHERE ANY OF THESE FAILED TO MATERIALIZE, FLORAL PATTERNS.

AT EASTER, DAD WOULD PAINT GOOSE EGGS WITH TWINING TEA ROSES.

DURING THE ENSUING HUNT, WE WOULD BE SURE TO FIND A YELLOW EGG IN A THATCH OF DAFFODILS, A LAVENDER EGG PASSING ITSELF OFF AS A CROCUS...

...AND NESTLED IN THE CRAB APPLE TREE, A PINK EGG THE PRECISE SHADE OF THE BLOSSOMS THAT WOULD SOON BURST FORTH THERE.

OUR GAMES OF BASEBALL--ALREADY LETHARGIC AFFAIRS--WOULD GRIND TO A HALT AS SOON AS THE BALL ROLLED NEAR A PERENNIAL BORDER.

DRAT.

THERE MY FATHER WOULD BECOME LOST TO US IN A REVERY OF WEEDING.

DAD, COME ON!

FORGET IT.

AT THE FUN HOME, DAD WOULD TAKE A BREAK FROM HIS GRISLY CHORES TO TWEAK THE STIFF ARRANGEMENTS DELIVERED BY THE FLORIST.

UGLY AS THESE WERE, THEIR QUICK, DAMP SCENT MASKED THE ODOR OF FORMALDEHYDE.

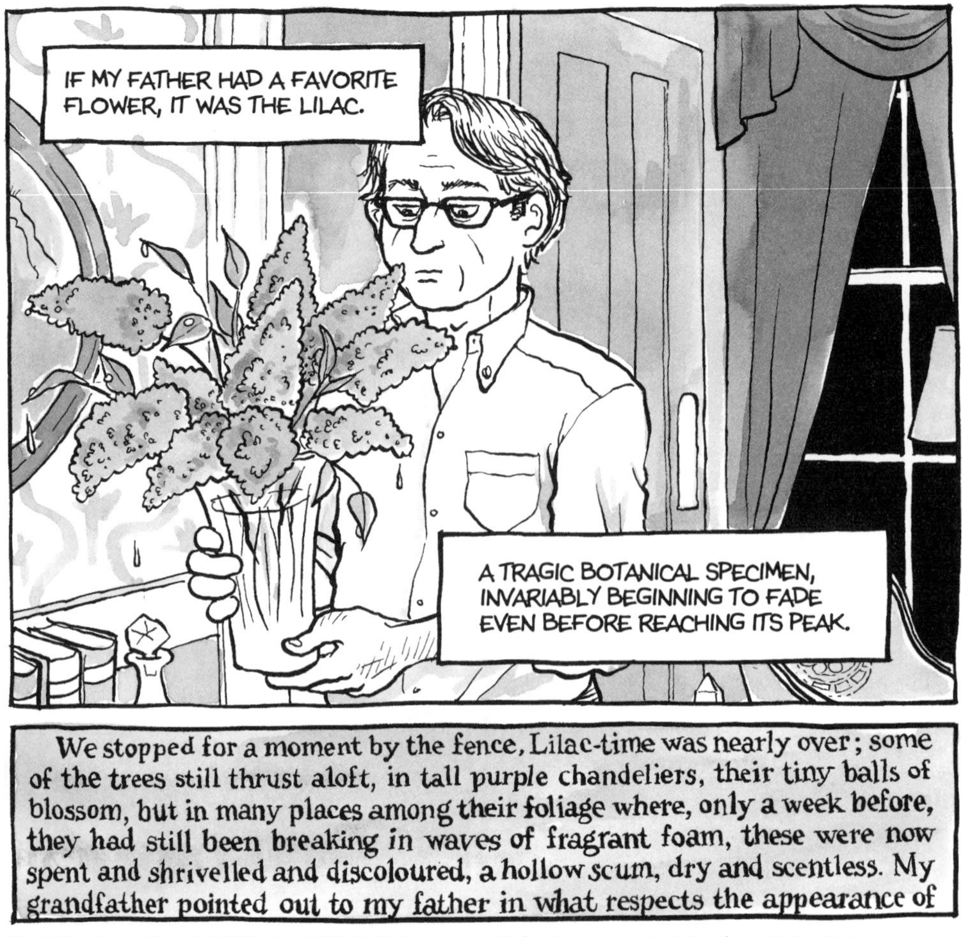
IF MY FATHER HAD A FAVORITE FLOWER, IT WAS THE LILAC.
A TRAGIC BOTANICAL SPECIMEN, INVARIABLY BEGINNING TO FADE EVEN BEFORE REACHING ITS PEAK.

We stopped for a moment by the fence, Lilac-time was nearly over; some of the trees still thrust aloft, in tall purple chandeliers, their tiny balls of blossom, but in many places among their foliage where, only a week before, they had still been breaking in waves of fragrant foam, these were now spent and shrivelled and discoloured, a hollow scum, dry and scentless. My grandfather pointed out to my father in what respects the appearance of

THAT'S HOW PROUST DESCRIBES THE LILACS BORDERING SWANN'S WAY IN *REMEMBRANCE OF THINGS PAST*.

MY FATHER, AS I SAY, HAD BEGUN READING THIS THE YEAR BEFORE HE DIED.

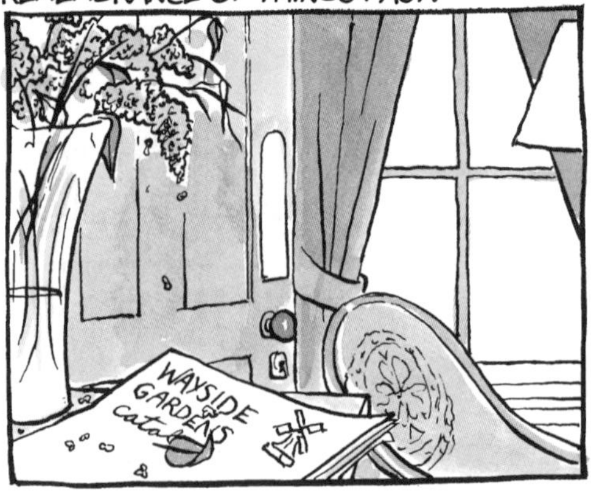
WAYSIDE GARDENS

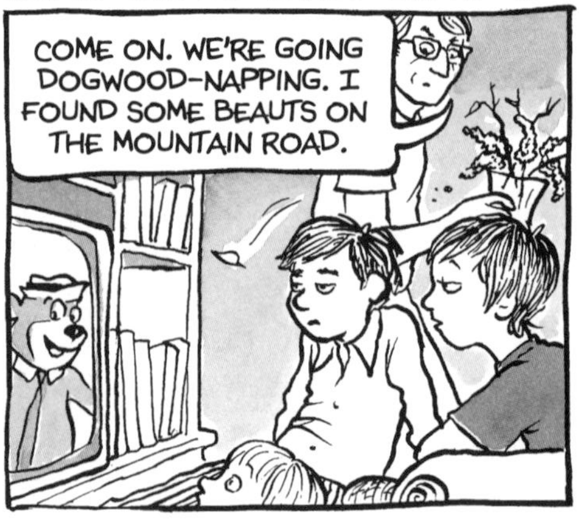
COME ON. WE'RE GOING DOGWOOD-NAPPING. I FOUND SOME BEAUTS ON THE MOUNTAIN ROAD.

AFTER THE LILAC PASSAGE, PROUST DESCRIBES SWANN'S GARDEN IN A FEAT OF BOTH LITERARY AND HORTICULTURAL VIRTUOSITY THAT CLIMAXES IN THE NARRATOR'S RAPTUROUS COMMUNION WITH THE PINK BLOSSOMS OF THE HAWTHORN HEDGE.

THROUGH THE HEDGE, PROUST'S NARRATOR COULD SEE EVEN DEEPER INTO SWANN'S GARDEN.

THERE, SURROUNDED BY JASMINE, VERBENA, AND PANSIES, SAT A LITTLE GIRL.

THE YOUNG NARRATOR, FAILING TO DISTINGUISH THIS GIRL, GILBERTE, FROM THE GENERAL FLORAL FECUNDITY, INSTANTLY FELL IN LOVE WITH HER.

93

PROUST WOULD HAVE INTENSE, EMOTIONAL FRIENDSHIPS WITH FASHIONABLE WOMEN...

...BUT IT WAS YOUNG, OFTEN STRAIGHT, MEN WITH WHOM HE FELL IN LOVE.

HE WOULD ALSO FICTIONALIZE REAL PEOPLE IN HIS LIFE BY TRANSPOSING THEIR GENDER--THE NARRATOR'S LOVER ALBERTINE, FOR EXAMPLE, IS OFTEN READ AS A PORTRAIT OF PROUST'S BELOVED CHAUFFEUR/SECRETARY, ALFRED.

MY FATHER COULD NOT AFFORD A CHAUFFEUR/SECRETARY.

BUT HE DID SPRING FOR THE OCCASIONAL YARDWORK ASSISTANT/BABYSITTER.

94

HE WOULD CULTIVATE THESE YOUNG MEN LIKE ORCHIDS.

I ADMIRED THEIR MASCULINE CHARMS MYSELF.

INDEED, I HAD BECOME A CONNOISSEUR OF MASCULINITY AT AN EARLY AGE.

I SENSED A CHINK IN MY FAMILY'S ARMOR, AN UNDEFENDED GAP IN THE CIRCLE OF OUR WAGONS WHICH CRIED OUT, IT SEEMED TO ME, FOR SOME PLAIN, TWO-FISTED SINEW.

I MEASURED MY FATHER AGAINST THE GRIMY DEER HUNTERS AT THE GAS STATION UPTOWN, WITH THEIR YELLOW WORKBOOTS AND SHORN-SHEEP HAIRCUTS.

ATLANTIC LUBRICATION WASHING

Stroehmann's SUNBEAM BREAD

THE EVER-PRESENT CHEW TIN

AND WHERE HE FELL SHORT, I STEPPED IN.

WHERE'S YOUR BARRETTE?

IT KEEPS THE HAIR OUT OF YOUR EYES.

SO WOULD A CREWCUT.

I COUNTED AS AN INDICATION OF MY SUCCESS THE NICKNAME BESTOWED ON ME BY MY OLDER COUSINS.

HEY, BUTCH! THINK FAST!

NO ONE NEEDED TO EXPLAIN WHAT IT MEANT.

IT WAS SELF-DESCRIPTIVE. CROPPED, CURT, PERCUSSIVE. PRACTICALLY ONOMATOPOEIC. AT ANY RATE, THE OPPOSITE OF SISSY.

AND DESPITE THE TYRANNICAL POWER WITH WHICH HE HELD SWAY, IT WAS CLEAR TO ME THAT MY FATHER WAS A BIG SISSY.

WHAT DID YOU DO WITH YOUR BARRETTE?

HEY THERE, GEORGY GIRL ♪

FORD

PROUST REFERS TO HIS EXPLICITLY HOMOSEXUAL CHARACTERS AS "INVERTS." I'VE ALWAYS BEEN FOND OF THIS ANTI-QUATED CLINICAL TERM.

IT FELL OUT!

I DON'T CARE! NEXT TIME I SEE YOU WITHOUT IT, I'LL WALE YOU.

OW!

IT'S IMPRECISE AND INSUFFICIENT, DEFINING THE HOMOSEXUAL AS A PERSON WHOSE GENDER EXPRESSION IS AT ODDS WITH HIS OR HER SEX.

BUT IN THE ADMITTEDLY LIMITED SAMPLE COMPRISING MY FATHER AND ME, PERHAPS IT IS SUFFICIENT.

(FIVE YEARS LATER)

NOT ONLY WERE WE INVERTS. WE WERE INVERSIONS OF ONE ANOTHER.

IT WAS A WAR OF CROSS-PURPOSES, AND SO DOOMED TO PERPETUAL ESCALATION.

BETWEEN US LAY A SLENDER DEMILITARIZED ZONE--OUR SHARED REVERENCE FOR MASCULINE BEAUTY.

BUT I WANTED THE MUSCLES AND TWEED LIKE MY FATHER WANTED THE VELVET AND PEARLS--SUBJECTIVELY, FOR MYSELF.

THE OBJECTS OF OUR DESIRE WERE QUITE DIFFERENT.

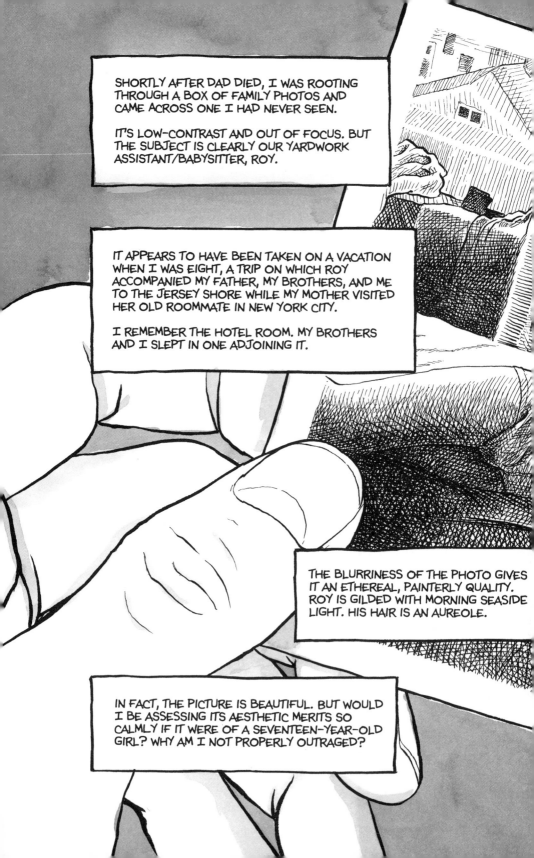

SHORTLY AFTER DAD DIED, I WAS ROOTING THROUGH A BOX OF FAMILY PHOTOS AND CAME ACROSS ONE I HAD NEVER SEEN.

IT'S LOW-CONTRAST AND OUT OF FOCUS. BUT THE SUBJECT IS CLEARLY OUR YARDWORK ASSISTANT/BABYSITTER, ROY.

IT APPEARS TO HAVE BEEN TAKEN ON A VACATION WHEN I WAS EIGHT, A TRIP ON WHICH ROY ACCOMPANIED MY FATHER, MY BROTHERS, AND ME TO THE JERSEY SHORE WHILE MY MOTHER VISITED HER OLD ROOMMATE IN NEW YORK CITY.

I REMEMBER THE HOTEL ROOM. MY BROTHERS AND I SLEPT IN ONE ADJOINING IT.

THE BLURRINESS OF THE PHOTO GIVES IT AN ETHEREAL, PAINTERLY QUALITY. ROY IS GILDED WITH MORNING SEASIDE LIGHT. HIS HAIR IS AN AUREOLE.

IN FACT, THE PICTURE IS BEAUTIFUL. BUT WOULD I BE ASSESSING ITS AESTHETIC MERITS SO CALMLY IF IT WERE OF A SEVENTEEN-YEAR-OLD GIRL? WHY AM I NOT PROPERLY OUTRAGED?

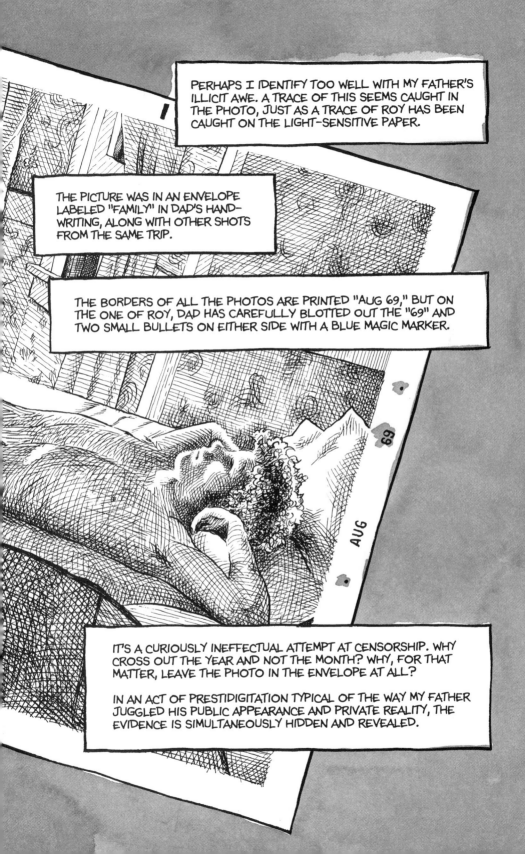

PERHAPS I IDENTIFY TOO WELL WITH MY FATHER'S ILLICIT AWE. A TRACE OF THIS SEEMS CAUGHT IN THE PHOTO, JUST AS A TRACE OF ROY HAS BEEN CAUGHT ON THE LIGHT-SENSITIVE PAPER.

THE PICTURE WAS IN AN ENVELOPE LABELED "FAMILY" IN DAD'S HAND-WRITING, ALONG WITH OTHER SHOTS FROM THE SAME TRIP.

THE BORDERS OF ALL THE PHOTOS ARE PRINTED "AUG 69," BUT ON THE ONE OF ROY, DAD HAS CAREFULLY BLOTTED OUT THE "69" AND TWO SMALL BULLETS ON EITHER SIDE WITH A BLUE MAGIC MARKER.

IT'S A CURIOUSLY INEFFECTUAL ATTEMPT AT CENSORSHIP. WHY CROSS OUT THE YEAR AND NOT THE MONTH? WHY, FOR THAT MATTER, LEAVE THE PHOTO IN THE ENVELOPE AT ALL?

IN AN ACT OF PRESTIDIGITATION TYPICAL OF THE WAY MY FATHER JUGGLED HIS PUBLIC APPEARANCE AND PRIVATE REALITY, THE EVIDENCE IS SIMULTANEOUSLY HIDDEN AND REVEALED.

A PERUSAL OF THE NEGATIVES REVEALS THREE BRIGHT SHOTS OF MY BROTHERS AND ME ON THE BEACH FOLLOWED BY THE DARK, MURKY ONE OF ROY ON THE BED.

IN ONE OF PROUST'S SWEEPING METAPHORS, THE TWO DIRECTIONS IN WHICH THE NARRATOR'S FAMILY CAN OPT FOR A WALK--SWANN'S WAY AND THE GUERMANTES WAY-- ARE INITIALLY PRESENTED AS DIAMETRICALLY OPPOSED.

BOURGEOIS VS. ARISTOCRATIC, HOMO VS. HETERO, CITY VS. COUNTRY, EROS VS. ART, PRIVATE VS. PUBLIC.

BUT AT THE END OF THE NOVEL THE TWO WAYS ARE REVEALED TO CONVERGE--TO HAVE ALWAYS CONVERGED--THROUGH A VAST "NETWORK OF TRANSVERSALS."

AFTER A FEW DAYS AT THE BEACH, WE DROVE TO NEW YORK TO PICK MOM UP.

WE'RE UNDER THE MIDDLE OF THE RIVER.

SHE WAS STAYING ON BLEECKER STREET WITH HER FRIEND ELLY.

ROY TOOK US FOR A WALK WHILE DAD WENT UP TO THE APARTMENT. IN THE HOT AUGUST AFTERNOON, THE CITY WAS REDUCED, LIKE A LONG-SIMMERING DEMIGLACE, TO A FRAGRANCE OF STUNNING RICHNESS AND COMPLEXITY.

I HAVE A HALLUCINOGENIC MEMORY OF A THROBBING WELTER OF PEOPLE IN A LARGE CIRCLE. IT MUST HAVE BEEN WASHINGTON SQUARE PARK.

MAYBE I WAS EXPERIENCING A CONTACT HIGH FROM THE LSD TRIPS NO DOUBT SWIRLING AROUND US.

OR PERHAPS IT WAS A CONTACT HIGH OF A DIFFERENT SORT. IT HAD ONLY BEEN A FEW WEEKS SINCE THE STONEWALL RIOTS, I REALIZE NOW.

AND WHILE I ACKNOWLEDGE THE ABSURDITY OF CLAIMING A CONNECTION TO THAT MYTHOLOGIZED FLASHPOINT...

We homosexuals plead with our people to please help maintain peaceful and quiet conduct on the streets of The Village. —Mattachine

...MIGHT NOT A LINGERING VIBRATION, A QUANTUM PARTICLE OF REBELLION, STILL HAVE HUNG IN THE HUMECTANT AIR?

AT THE VERY LEAST, THIS AFTERNOON IS A CURIOUS WATERSHED BETWEEN MY PARENTS' YOUNG ADULTHOOD IN THE CITY A DECADE EARLIER, AND MY OWN A DECADE LATER.

I IMAGINE MY FATHER TAKING THE BUS UP FROM COLLEGE TO VISIT MY MOTHER, WALKING DOWN CHRISTOPHER STREET IN HIS BORROWED BROOKS BROTHERS FINERY.

HOW MUCH DID MY MOTHER'S MILIEU FACTOR INTO HIS ATTRACTION?

HAD HE SOMEHOW CONFLATED HER WITH HER ADDRESS, LIKE PROUST'S NARRATOR HAD WITH GILBERTE AND THE GARDEN?

I'VE NEVER BEEN INSIDE THE FRONT DOOR OF MOM'S OLD BUILDING, BUT I'M AS NOSTALGIC ABOUT IT AS IF I'D LIVED THERE MYSELF.

WHERE WAS YOUR APARTMENT?

4-E, UP THERE.

ON SUCCESSIVE VISITS TO THE CITY, I GREW TO KNOW THE NEIGHBORHOOD.

THIS IS CHUMLEY'S. DAD AND I USED TO COME DRINK HERE.

IT'S A BAR? HOW COME THERE'S NO SIGN?

YOU JUST HAVE TO KNOW ABOUT IT.

NEAT.

YEARS LATER, ON AN EVENING OF BAR-HOPPING, I ENTERED THIS ESTABLISH-MENT WITH A GANG OF LESBIAN FRIENDS.

COVER'S FIFTEEN DOLLARS, LADIES.

FIFTEEN DOLLARS?!

WE LEFT, TOO NAIVE TO REALIZE WE'D BEEN EIGHTY-SIXED. I DIDN'T EVEN KNOW THE TERM *EIGHTY-SIX*. WHEN I DID LEARN IT, MY RETROACTIVE MORTIFICATION WAS SOFTENED BY THE KNOWLEDGE THAT I'D TAKEN PART IN SUCH A LEXICOGRAPHICAL EVENT.

by this gun. **3.** *Slang* A piano. [Sense 3, from keys. **eight·y·six** or **86** (ā'tē-sĭks') *tr.v.* **eight·y·sixed, eight·y·six·ing, eight·y·six·es** or **86·ed. 86·ing, 86·es** *Slang* **1.** To refuse to serve (an unwelcome customer) at a bar or restaurant. **2a.** To throw out; eject. **b.** To throw away; discard. [Perhaps after Chumley's bar and restaurant at 86 Bedford Street in Greenwich Village, New York City.] **-ein** *suff.* A chemical compound related to a specified compound with

THERE WERE MANY SUCH HUMILIATIONS IN STORE FOR ME AS A YOUNG LESBIAN.

HI!

I'D COME TO NEW YORK AFTER COLLEGE, EXPECTING A BOHEMIAN REFUGE...

YEAH, YOU.

UM...THAT WAS VERY BRAVE OF YOU. I'VE NEVER HAD THE NERVE TO APPROACH ANYONE IN HERE.

...BUT THE VILLAGE IN THE EARLY EIGHTIES WAS A COLD, MERCENARY PLACE.

OH, I'M USED TO IT. HERE, I'D LIKE TO INVITE YOU TO A RADICAL WOMEN MEETING. ARE YOU FAMILIAR WITH US?

ONCE, MY MOTHER SHARED A GLIMPSE OF LIFE THERE IN THE OLD DAYS.

WE USED TO HEAR LESBIANS FIGHTING DOWN ON THE STREET OUTSIDE THE BARS. WE THOUGHT IT WAS SO FUNNY AND SAD.

WOW.

GOYA

BROOKLYN

IF HER COMMENT WAS AN ATTEMPT TO SWAY ME FROM MY COURSE, IT FAILED UTTERLY. I BECAME FASCINATED WITH LESBIAN PULP FICTION FROM THE FIFTIES--THE BAR RAIDS AND THE ILLEGAL CROSS-DRESSING.

IF THE COPS SEARCHED ME, COULD I PASS THE THREE-ARTICLES-OF-WOMEN'S-CLOTHING RULE?

WOMEN IN THE SHADOWS

WOULD I HAVE HAD THE GUTS TO BE ONE OF THOSE EISENHOWER-ERA BUTCHES?

OR WOULD I HAVE MARRIED AND SOUGHT SUCCOR FROM MY HIGH SCHOOL STUDENTS?

IN DAD'S EDITION OF PROUST, THE TITLE OF VOLUME FOUR IS CHASTELY TRANSLATED AS *CITIES OF THE PLAIN* FROM THE FRENCH *SODOME ET GOMORRHE* .

THE ORIGINAL TITLE OF VOLUME TWO IS *À L'OMBRE DES JEUNES FILLES EN FLEURS*, LITERALLY "IN THE SHADOW OF YOUNG GIRLS IN FLOWER."

THEY FOLD BACK, AND YOU HAVE TO CLOSE THEM WITH CUFFLINKS.

THE TRANSLATION TO *WITHIN A BUDDING GROVE* SHIFTS THE EMPHASIS PRIMLY FROM THE EROTIC TO THE BOTANICAL.

AND *BUDDING* IS THE ONLY POSSIBLE WORD TO DESCRIBE THE PAINFUL, ITCHY BEGINNINGS OF MY BREASTS, AT TWELVE.

BUT OF COURSE, AS PROUST HIMSELF SO LAVISHLY ILLUSTRATES, EROS AND BOTANY ARE PRETTY MUCH THE SAME THING.

I WANT A CUSTOM-MADE SHIRT. WITH FRENCH CUFFS.

LADYSLIPPER

Wayside Gardens

Custom SHIRTMAKERS

IT'S TRUE I HAD NOT WANTED TO GROW BREASTS, BUT IT NEVER OCCURRED TO ME THAT THEY WOULD HURT.

NOR HAD I EXPECTED THEM TO BE SO ODDLY CARTILAGINOUS. ACCIDENTAL IMPACT WAS EXCRUCIATING.

SWOLLEN

TENDER

WHEN I WAS TEN, TWO YEARS AFTER OUR SEASIDE JAUNT WITH ROY, MY FATHER HAD FOUND SOMEONE NEW TO HELP WITH THE YARDWORK.

SO INSTEAD OF GOING TO THE BEACH, WE WENT CAMPING.

THE PLAN WAS TO GO TO OUR FAMILY'S DEER CAMP, CALLED THE BULLPEN.

THE BULLPEN WAS OUT IN THE FOREST OF THE ALLEGHENY PLATEAU, WHICH ONCE STRETCHED UNDIFFERENTIATED ALL THE WAY TO LAKE ERIE.

I DON'T LIKE THE WOODS.

I'M GONNA GO GET THE KEY FROM UNCLE FRED.

ME TOO.

OH, AND, BRUCE, CAN YOU TAKE THIS WITH YOU? IF ELSIE FINDS IT SHE'LL HAVE MY HIDE.

NOW IT WAS GOUGED WITH VAST STRIP MINES. MY BROTHERS AND I WERE EXCITED ABOUT SEEING THE MONSTROUS SHOVELS THAT TORE OFF WHOLE MOUNTAINTOPS.

THERE'S SOME MINING GOING ON JUST DOWN THE ROAD. BIG AS HOUSES, THOSE RIGS.

WHAT IS THIS?

DON'T OPEN IT. IT'S DIRTY. I'LL BE RIGHT BACK.

SPOTTS' MARKET

IT LOOKED CLEAN ENOUGH TO ME.

OH.

Kelly Plumbing & Heating

JANUARY 1971

I FELT AS IF I'D BEEN STRIPPED NAKED MYSELF, INEXPLICABLY ASHAMED, LIKE ADAM AND EVE.

ONCE WE WERE AT THE BULLPEN, MY BROTHERS DISCOVERED THE CALENDAR.

POLE FOR HANGING DEER

THAT AFTERNOON, WE DROVE OUT TO THE STRIP MINE.

THE SHOVEL WASN'T RUNNING, BUT THE OPERATOR LET US INTO THE CAB.

INSIDE I WAS ASTONISHED BY WHAT STRUCK ME AS A BIZARRE COINCIDENCE.

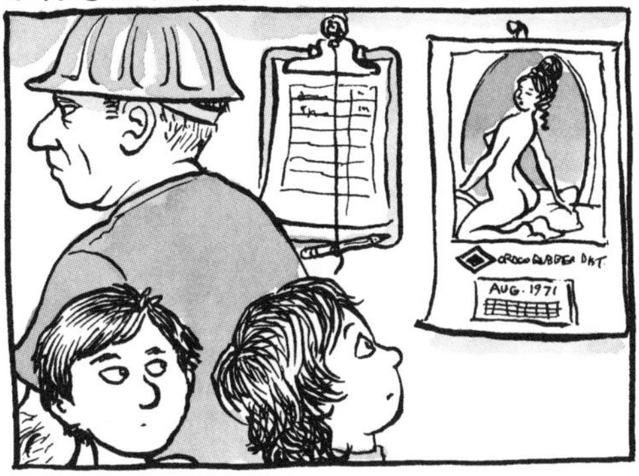
AUG. 1971

AS THE MAN SHOWED US AROUND, IT SEEMED IMPERATIVE THAT HE NOT KNOW I WAS A GIRL.

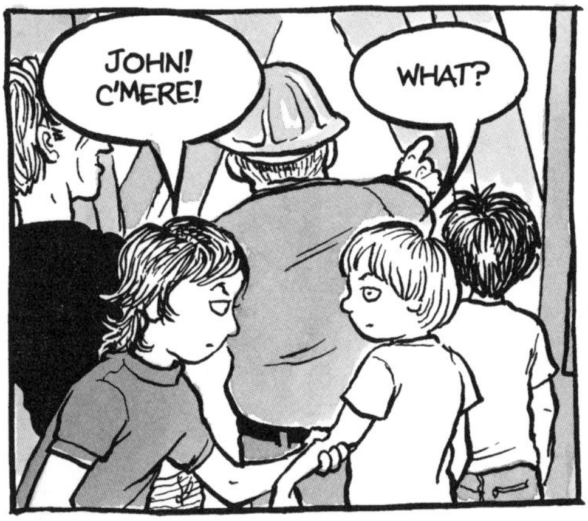
JOHN! C'MERE!
WHAT?

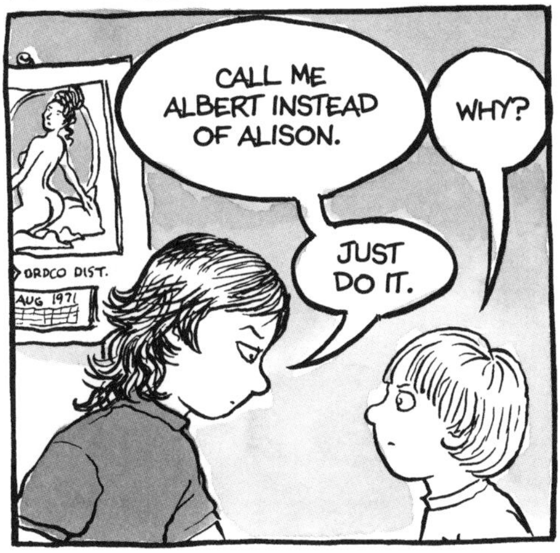
CALL ME ALBERT INSTEAD OF ALISON.
WHY?
JUST DO IT.
ORDCO DIST.
AUG 1971

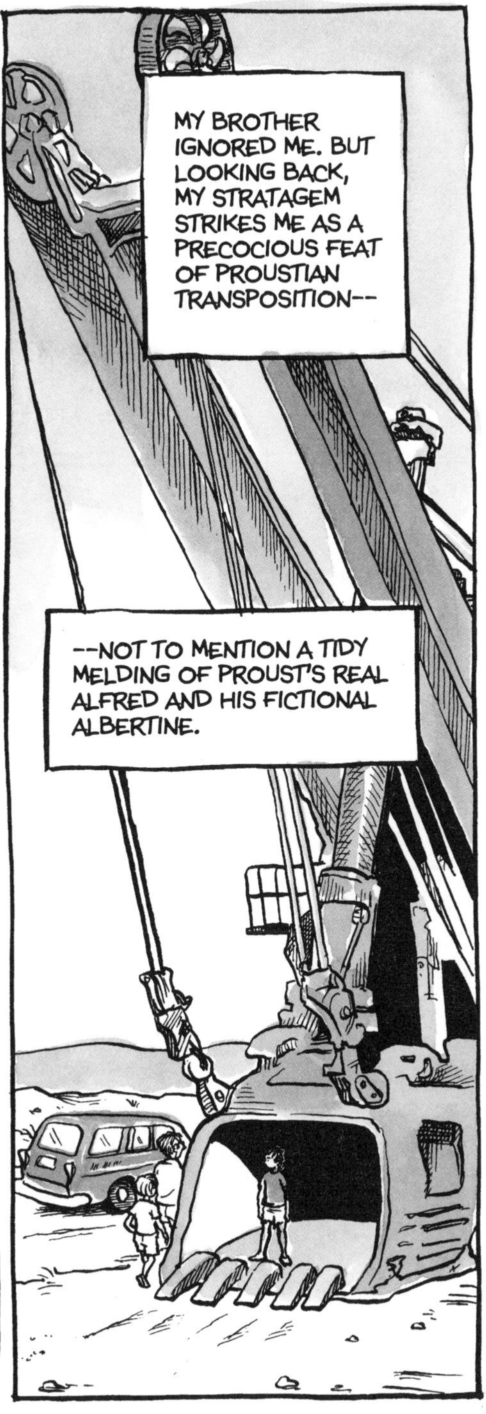
MY BROTHER IGNORED ME. BUT LOOKING BACK, MY STRATAGEM STRIKES ME AS A PRECOCIOUS FEAT OF PROUSTIAN TRANSPOSITION--
--NOT TO MENTION A TIDY MELDING OF PROUST'S REAL ALFRED AND HIS FICTIONAL ALBERTINE.

THE NEXT DAY, DAD WENT BACK TO TOWN FOR A FUNERAL. BILL SHOWED MY BROTHERS AND ME HOW TO SHOOT HIS .22. NONE OF US COULD MANAGE TO PULL THE TRIGGER.

ABASHED, WE SLUNK INTO THE WOODS TO GET CANS OF POP FROM THE SPRING.

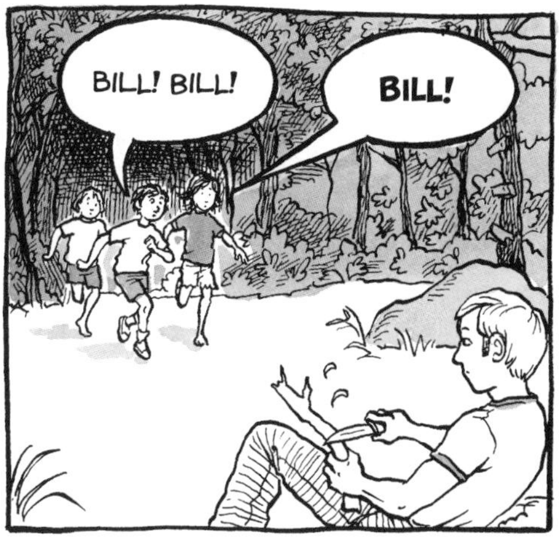
BILL! BILL!
BILL!

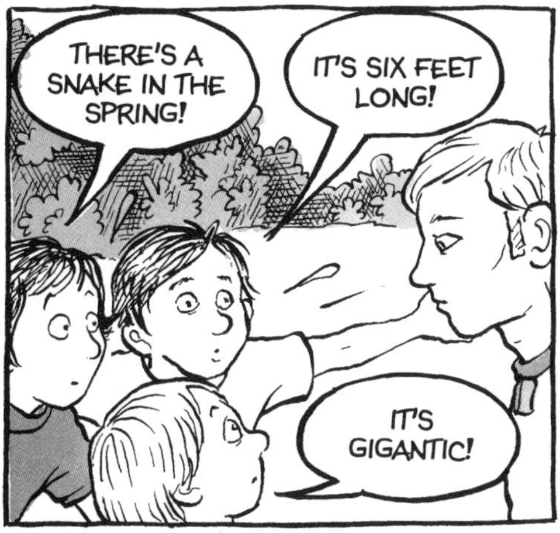
THERE'S A SNAKE IN THE SPRING!
IT'S SIX FEET LONG!
IT'S GIGANTIC!

I WAS SHOCKED WHEN BILL GRABBED THE GUN.

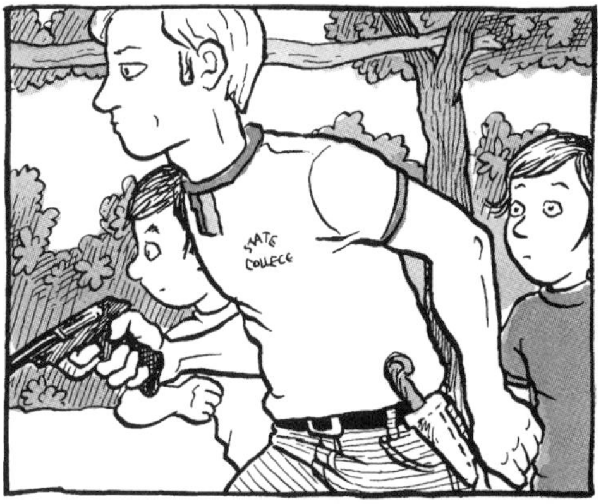
STATE COLLEGE

THEN RELIEVED AND SOMEWHAT EMBARRASSED THAT THE SNAKE WAS GONE.

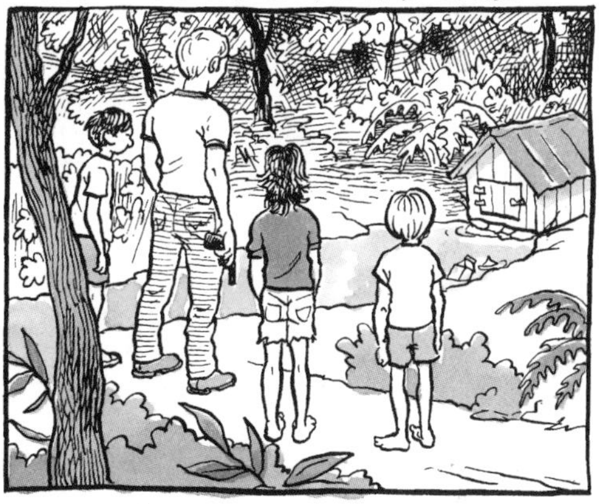

ON THE DRIVE HOME, A POSTLAPSARIAN MELANCHOLY CREPT OVER ME. I HAD FAILED SOME UNSPOKEN INITIATION RITE, AND LIFE'S POSSIBILITIES WERE NO LONGER INFINITE.

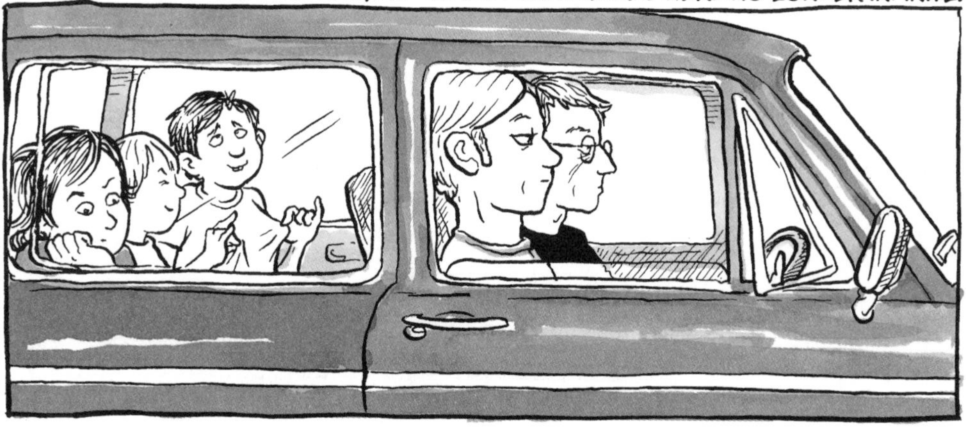

WHAT IF MY FATHER HAD SEEN A SNAKE THE SIZE OF THAT ONE?

THE SERPENT IS A VEXINGLY AMBIGUOUS ARCHETYPE.

IT'S OBVIOUSLY A PHALLUS, YET A MORE ANCIENT AND UNIVERSAL SYMBOL OF THE FEMININE PRINCIPLE WOULD BE HARD TO COME BY.

IT WAS --IT WAS DRINKING!

IT WAS HUGE!

PERHAPS THIS UNDIFFERENTIATION, THIS NONDUALITY, IS THE POINT.

BATHS. NOW.

MAYBE THAT'S WHAT'S SO UNSETTLING ABOUT SNAKES.

SEE? THIS IS HOW YOU'D LOOK IF YOU HAD LONG HAIR AND PULLED IT BACK IN A PONYTAIL.

MOMMM!

THEY ALSO IMPLY CYCLICALITY, LIFE FROM DEATH, CREATION FROM DESTRUCTION.

GOOD NIGHT.

THE WORM OUROBOROS EDDISON

AND IN A WAY, YOU COULD SAY THAT MY FATHER'S END WAS MY BEGINNING.

OR MORE PRECISELY, THAT THE END OF HIS LIE COINCIDED WITH THE BEGINNING OF MY TRUTH.

BECAUSE I'D BEEN LYING TOO, FOR A LONG TIME. SINCE I WAS FOUR OR FIVE.

DAD HAD TAKEN ME WITH HIM ON A BUSINESS TRIP TO PHILADELPHIA.

IN THE CITY, IN A LUNCHEONETTE...

...WE SAW A MOST UNSETTLING SIGHT.

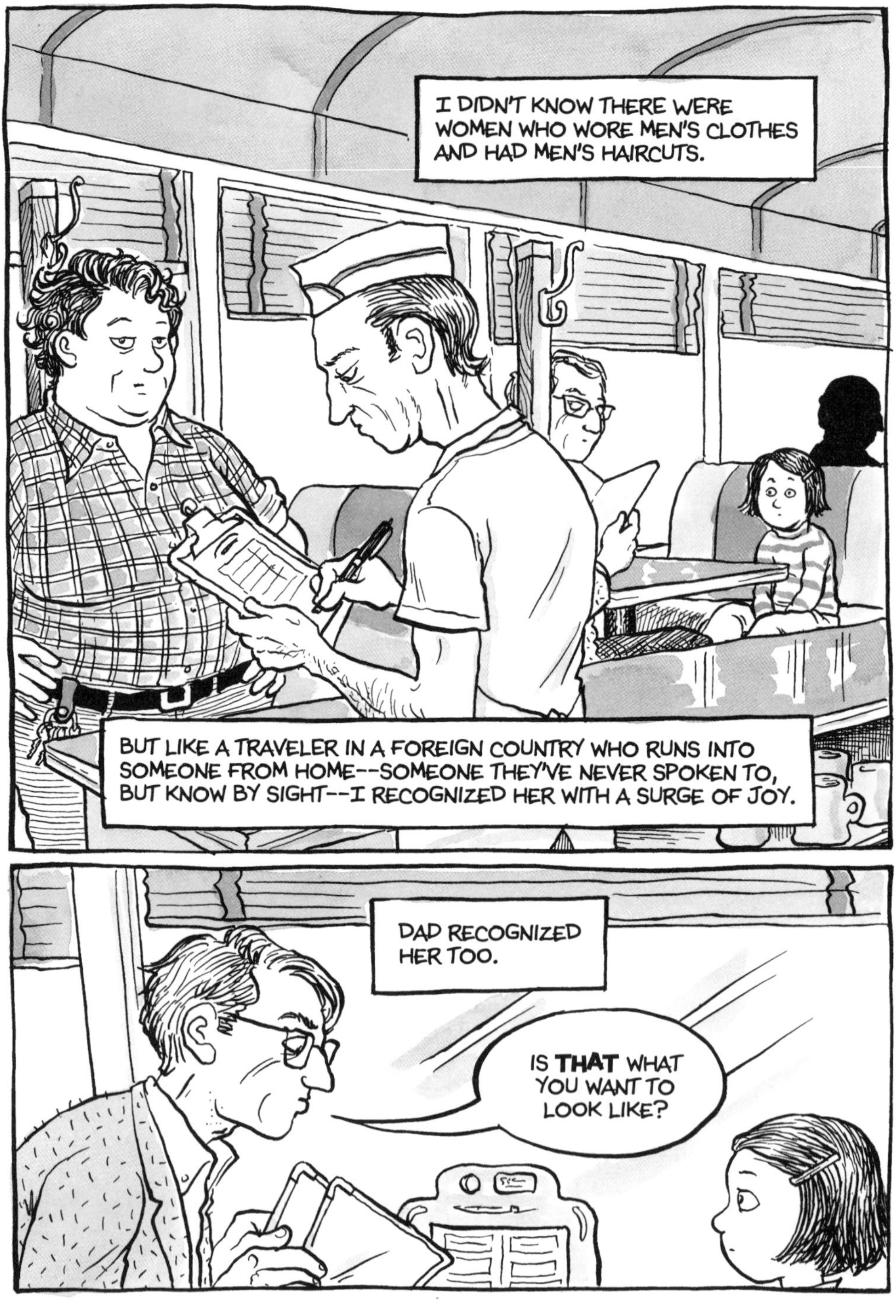
I DIDN'T KNOW THERE WERE WOMEN WHO WORE MEN'S CLOTHES AND HAD MEN'S HAIRCUTS.
BUT LIKE A TRAVELER IN A FOREIGN COUNTRY WHO RUNS INTO SOMEONE FROM HOME--SOMEONE THEY'VE NEVER SPOKEN TO, BUT KNOW BY SIGHT--I RECOGNIZED HER WITH A SURGE OF JOY.
DAD RECOGNIZED HER TOO.
IS **THAT** WHAT YOU WANT TO LOOK LIKE?

WHAT ELSE COULD I SAY?

BUT THE VISION OF THE TRUCK-DRIVING BULLDYKE SUSTAINED ME THROUGH THE YEARS...

...AS PERHAPS IT HAUNTED MY FATHER.

AFTER DAD DIED, AN UPDATED TRANSLATION OF PROUST CAME OUT. *REMEMBRANCE OF THINGS PAST* WAS RE-TITLED *IN SEARCH OF LOST TIME.*

THE NEW TITLE IS A MORE LITERAL TRANSLATION OF *À LA RECHERCHE DU TEMPS PERDU,* BUT IT STILL DOESN'T QUITE CAPTURE THE FULL RESONANCE OF *PERDU.*

WHAT'S LOST IN TRANSLATION IS THE COMPLEXITY OF LOSS ITSELF. IN THE SAME BOX WHERE I FOUND THE PHOTO OF ROY, THERE'S ONE OF DAD AT ABOUT THE SAME AGE.

HE'S WEARING A WOMEN'S BATHING SUIT. A FRATERNITY PRANK? BUT THE POSE HE STRIKES IS NOT MINCING OR SILLY AT ALL.

HE'S LISSOME, ELEGANT.

IN ANOTHER PICTURE, HE'S SUNBATHING ON THE TARPAPER ROOF OF HIS FRAT HOUSE JUST AFTER HE TURNED TWENTY-TWO. WAS THE BOY WHO TOOK IT HIS LOVER?

AS THE GIRL WHO TOOK THIS POLAROID OF ME ON A FIRE ESCAPE ON MY TWENTY-FIRST BIRTHDAY WAS MINE?

THE EXTERIOR SETTING, THE PAINED GRIN, THE FLEXIBLE WRISTS, EVEN THE ANGLE OF SHADOW FALLING ACROSS OUR FACES--IT'S ABOUT AS CLOSE AS A TRANSLATION CAN GET.

CHAPTER 5

THE CANARY-COLORED
CARAVAN OF DEATH

TWO NIGHTS BEFORE MY FATHER DIED, I DREAMED THAT I WAS OUT AT THE BULLPEN WITH HIM. THERE WAS A GLORIOUS SUNSET VISIBLE THROUGH THE TREES.

DAD! C'MON! LET'S GO UP THE HILL AND SEE IT!

AT FIRST HE IGNORED ME. I RACED OVER THE VELVETY MOSS IN MY BARE FEET.

HURRY UP! IT'S AMAZING!

WHEN HE FINALLY GOT THERE, THE SUN HAD SUNK BEHIND THE HORIZON AND THE BRILLIANT COLORS WERE GONE.

YOU **MISSED** IT! GOD, IT WAS **BEAUTIFUL!**

IF THIS WAS A PREMONITORY DREAM, I CAN ONLY SAY THAT ITS CONDOLENCE-CARD ASSOCIATION OF DEATH WITH A SETTING SUN IS MAUDLIN IN THE EXTREME.

YET MY FATHER DID POSSESS A CERTAIN RADIANCE--

--PERHAPS DUE TO HIS HABIT OF EXCESSIVE, EVEN IDOLATROUS, SUNBATHING--

OFF TO CHURCH

--AND SO HIS DEATH HAD AN INEVITABLY DIMMING, CREPUSCULAR EFFECT. MY COUSIN EVEN POSTPONED HIS ANNUAL FIREWORKS DISPLAY THE NIGHT BEFORE THE FUNERAL.

WHY?

WELL, UH...OUT OF RESPECT FOR YOUR DAD.

I HAD BEEN HOPING FOR A MORE BLUNT RESPONSE, LIKE, "BECAUSE YOUR FATHER JUST DIED, YOU IDIOT."

MY NUMBNESS, ALONG WITH ALL THE MEALY-MOUTHED MOURNING, WAS MAKING ME IRRITABLE. WHAT WOULD HAPPEN IF WE SPOKE THE TRUTH?

I DIDN'T FIND OUT.

WHEN I THINK ABOUT HOW MY FATHER'S STORY MIGHT HAVE TURNED OUT DIFFERENTLY, A GEOGRAPHICAL RELOCATION IS USUALLY INVOLVED.

BEECH CREEK — Bruce Bechdel, 44, of Maple Avenue, Beech Creek, well-known funeral director and high school teacher, died of multiple injuries suffered when he was struck by a tractor-trailer along Route 150, about two miles north of Beech Creek at 11:10 a.m. Wednesday.

He was pronounced dead on arrival at Lock Haven Hospital while standing on the berm, police said.

Bechdel was born in Beech Creek on April 8, 1936 and was the son of Dorothy Bechdel Bechdel, who survives and lives in Beech Creek, and the late Claude H. Bechdel.

He operated the Bruce A. Bechdel Funeral Home in Beech Creek and was also an English teacher at Bald Eagle-Nittany

Institute of Mortuary Science.

He served in the U.S. Army in Germany.

Bechdel was president of the Clinton County Historical Society and was instrumental in the restoration of the Heisey Museum after the 1972 flood and in 1978 he and his wife, the former Helen Fontana, received the annual Clinton County Historical Society preservation ... the work at their 10- ...ctorian house in Beech

IF ONLY HE'D BEEN ABLE TO ESCAPE THE GRAVITATIONAL TUG OF BEECH CREEK, I TELL MYSELF, HIS PARTICULAR SUN MIGHT NOT HAVE SET IN SO PRECIPITATE A MANNER.

gardening and stepped onto the roadway. He was struck by the right front portion of the truck

degree from The Pennsylvania State University. He was also a graduate of the Pittsburgh

...s a member of the ...n Society of America, ...d of directors of the ...k Playhouse, National Council of Teachers of English, Phi Kappa Psi fraternity and was a deacon at the Blanchard

PERHAPS THE PECULIAR TOPOGRAPHY REALLY DID EXERT SOME KIND OF PULL.

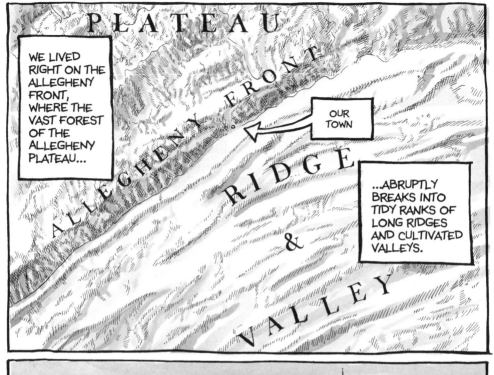

WE LIVED RIGHT ON THE ALLEGHENY FRONT, WHERE THE VAST FOREST OF THE ALLEGHENY PLATEAU...

OUR TOWN

...ABRUPTLY BREAKS INTO TIDY RANKS OF LONG RIDGES AND CULTIVATED VALLEYS.

PLATEAU

ALLEGHENY FRONT

RIDGE & VALLEY

THE APPALACHIAN RIDGES--MANY LONGER THAN HADRIAN'S WALL--HISTORICALLY DISCOURAGED CULTURAL EXCHANGE. MY GRANDMOTHER, FOR EXAMPLE, WAS A BECHDEL EVEN BEFORE SHE MARRIED MY GRANDFATHER. AND IN OUR TOWN OF 800 SOULS, THERE WERE 26 BECHDEL FAMILIES LISTED IN THE PHONE BOOK.

THIS DESPITE THE FACT THAT PEOPLE COULD EASILY DRIVE AROUND THE MOUNTAINS BY THE TIME MY FATHER WAS A CHILD.

DAD

AND BY THE TIME OF MY OWN CHILDHOOD, THEY COULD DRIVE EVEN MORE EASILY RIGHT ACROSS THEM.

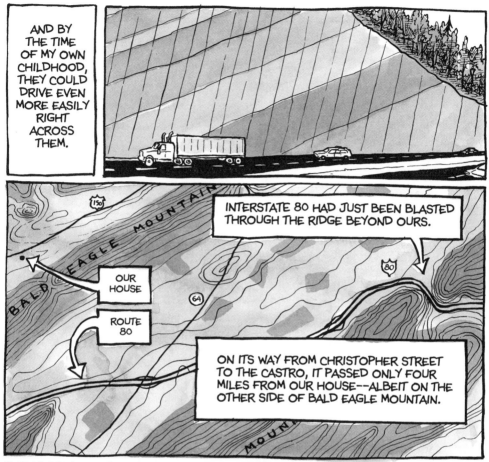

INTERSTATE 80 HAD JUST BEEN BLASTED THROUGH THE RIDGE BEYOND OURS.

BALD EAGLE MOUNTAIN

OUR HOUSE

ROUTE 80

ON ITS WAY FROM CHRISTOPHER STREET TO THE CASTRO, IT PASSED ONLY FOUR MILES FROM OUR HOUSE--ALBEIT ON THE OTHER SIDE OF BALD EAGLE MOUNTAIN.

MOUN

THIS MASSIVE EARTHEN BERM EFFECTIVELY DEADENED ANY HINT OF NOISE FROM THE GLORIOUS THOROUGHFARE...

...EXCEPT ON STILL, HOT NIGHTS WHEN THE HUMIDITY WAS PARTICULARLY CONDUCTIVE.

OUR SUN ROSE OVER BALD EAGLE MOUNTAIN'S HAZY BLUE FLANK.

(WE SAW LOTS OF SUNRISES IN 1974, THANKS TO THE ENERGY CRISIS AND THE YEAR-ROUND DAYLIGHT SAVINGS TIME IT ENTAILED.)

AND IT SET BEHIND THE STRIP MINE-POCKED PLATEAU...

...TYPICALLY WITH SOME DEGREE OF PYROTECHNIC SPLENDOR, DUE TO PARTICULATES FROM THE PRE-CLEAN AIR ACT PAPER MILL TEN MILES AWAY.

WITH SIMILAR PERVERSITY, THE SPARKLING CREEK THAT COURSED DOWN FROM THE PLATEAU AND THROUGH OUR TOWN WAS CRYSTAL CLEAR PRECISELY BECAUSE IT WAS POLLUTED.

MINE RUNOFF HAD LEFT THE WATER TOO ACIDIC TO SUPPORT LIFE OF ANY KIND.

WADING IN THIS FISHLESS CREEK AND SWOONING AT THE SALMON SKY, I LEARNED FIRSTHAND THAT MOST ELEMENTAL OF ALL IRONIES.

THAT, AS WALLACE STEVENS PUT IT IN MOM'S FAVORITE POEM, "DEATH IS THE MOTHER OF BEAUTY."

I WAS INSPIRED TO POETRY MYSELF BY THESE PICTURESQUE SURROUNDINGS, AT THE AGE OF SEVEN.

SPRING
spring is very nice youknow not a bit of ice or snow!

I SHOWED IT TO MY FATHER, WHO IMPROVISED A SECOND STANZA ON THE SPOT.

LILACS, TULIPS, AND DAFFODILS PEEK THEIR HEADS O'ER THE WINDOWSILLS.

LIMP WITH ADMIRATION, I ADDED HIS LINES TO MY TYPESCRIPT....

...THEN ILLUSTRATED THE PAGE WITH A MUDDY WATERCOLOR SUNSET.

IN THE FOREGROUND STANDS A MAN, MY SAD PROXY, GAZING ON THE UNTIMELY ECLIPSE OF HIS CREATIVE LIGHT.

WE HAD A HUGE, OVERSIZE COLORING BOOK OF E.H. SHEPARD'S ILLUSTRATIONS FOR *THE WIND IN THE WILLOWS*.

SPRING
spring is very nice youknow
not a bit of ice or snow!
LiLACS tu lips and daffodils
peak their heads inthewindowsill.

I NEVER WROTE ANOTHER POEM. AND SOON, I ABANDONED COLOR TOO.

DAD HAD READ ME BITS OF THE STORY FROM THE REAL BOOK. IN ONE SCENE, THE CHARMING SOCIOPATH MR. TOAD PURCHASES A GYPSY CARAVAN.

I WAS FILLING THIS IN ONE DAY WITH MY FAVORITE COLOR, MIDNIGHT BLUE.

WHAT ARE YOU DOING? THAT'S THE *CANARY-COLORED CARAVAN!*

IT WAS A CRAYONIC TOUR DE FORCE.

MY MOTHER'S TALENTS WERE NO LESS DAUNTING. ONCE I WENT WITH HER TO A HOUSE WHERE SHE ARGUED WITH A STRANGE MAN, AS IF SHE KNEW HIM INTIMATELY.

THIS WAS ACTING.

SHE COULD ALSO PLAY ASTONISHING THINGS ON THE PIANO, EVEN THE MUSIC FROM THE DOWNY COMMERCIAL ON TV.

SEVERAL YEARS AFTER DAD DIED, MOM WAS USING OUR OLD TAPE RECORDER TO REHEARSE FOR A PLAY. SHE READ FROM THE SCRIPT, LEAVING PAUSES WHERE IT WAS HER CHARACTER'S TURN TO SPEAK.

WHEN SHE CHECKED TO MAKE SURE THE MACHINE WAS RECORDING PROPERLY...

...SHE REALIZED THAT SHE WAS TAPING OVER MY FATHER'S VOICE.

THIS OWNER CHANGED THE ROOFS, THE PORCHES, THE CHIMNEYS, THE FIREPLACES, THE WALLS, THE WOODWORK, UNTIL IT BECAME A STYLISH TOWN HOUSE SUITABLE FOR A PROSPEROUS LAWYER'S FAMILY.

HE'S NOT TALKING ABOUT OUR HOUSE. HE'S PREPARING A GUIDED TOUR OF A MUSEUM RUN BY THE COUNTY HISTORICAL SOCIETY, OF WHICH HE WAS PRESIDENT.

IT'S JARRING TO HEAR MY FATHER SPEAK FROM BEYOND THE GRAVE.

PROCEEDING TO THE EAST PARLOR, WITH ITS BOLDLY SCROLLED ROCOCO PAPERS AND ITS BORDERED WALL-TO-WALL CARPET, YOU WILL SEE THE SHOWPLACE ROOM OF THE HOUSE.

SYNCHRO START

1

BUT THE MOST ARRESTING THING ABOUT THE TAPE IS ITS EVIDENCE OF BOTH MY PARENTS AT WORK, INTENT AND SEPARATE.

...RUB HER BACK FOR HER. **KKKKLICK**...AND SMALL, MULLIONED WINDOWS...

BASS RETURN

THEIR RAPT IMMERSION EVOKES A FAMILIAR RESENTMENT IN ME.

I'M HUNGRY!

I'LL MAKE LUNCH IN FIFTEEN MINUTES.

IT'S CHILDISH, PERHAPS, TO GRUDGE THEM THE SUSTENANCE OF THEIR CREATIVE SOLITUDE.

BUT IT WAS *ALL* THAT SUSTAINED THEM, AND WAS THUS ALL-CONSUMING.

FROM THEIR EXAMPLE, I LEARNED QUICKLY TO FEED MYSELF.

IT WAS A VICIOUS CIRCLE, THOUGH. THE MORE GRATIFICATION WE FOUND IN OUR OWN GENIUSES, THE MORE ISOLATED WE GREW.

OUR HOME WAS LIKE AN ARTISTS' COLONY. WE ATE TOGETHER, BUT OTHERWISE WERE ABSORBED IN OUR SEPARATE PURSUITS.

AND IN THIS ISOLATION, OUR CREATIVITY TOOK ON AN ASPECT OF COMPULSION.

MY ACTUAL OBSESSIVE-COMPULSIVE DISORDER BEGAN WHEN I WAS TEN.

> 19...20. 21, 22, 23...

FIRST IT INVOLVED A LOT OF COUNTING. TRYING TO MANIP-ULATE THE SLIGHTLY LEAKY BATHTUB FAUCET WITH MY TOE SO THAT IT WOULD STOP ON AN EVEN NUMBER OF DRIPS.

ODD NUMBERS AND MULTIPLES OF THIRTEEN WERE TO BE AVOIDED AT ALL COSTS.

> 24, 25...**26?!** 27, 28...

IF THESE FAILED TO ADD UP TO AN EVEN NUMBER, I'D INCLUDE ANOTHER SUBDIVISION, PERHAPS THE SMALL GROOVES IN THE METAL STRIP.

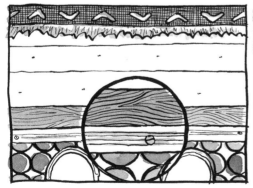

CROSSING THRESHOLDS BECAME A TIME-CONSUMING PROCEDURE SINCE I HAD TO TABULATE THE NUMBER OF EDGES OF FLOORING I SAW THERE.

THEN CAME THE INVISIBLE SUBSTANCE THAT HUNG IN DOORWAYS, AND THAT, I SOON REALIZED, HUNG LIKE SWAGS OF DRAPERY BETWEEN ALL SOLID OBJECTS.

THIS HAD TO BE GATHERED AND DIS-PERSED CONSTANTLY, TO KEEP IT AWAY FROM MY BODY--TO AVOID IN PARTIC-ULAR INHALING OR SWALLOWING IT.

DESPITE MY UNRELENTING VIGILANCE, THESE EFFORTS FELL SHORT. ODD NUMBERS AND MULTIPLES OF THIRTEEN WERE EVERYWHERE.

AND FESTOONS OF THE NOXIOUS SUBSTANCE PROLIFERATED BEYOND MY CONTROL. SO MY PREVENTIVE MEASURES SPAWNED MORE STOPGAP MEASURES.

IF I HADN'T SUCCESSFULLY NAVIGATED A DOORWAY, FOR EXAMPLE, I COULD RECITE A SPECIAL INCANTATION.

ENDORA! TURN ME BACK THIS INSTANT!

AND TO ENSURE THAT THE INCANTATION WOULD BE EFFECTIVE, I COULD REPEAT IT, THIS TIME WITH HAND GESTURES.

MOMM! SHE'S DOIN' IT!

IF MY DAY WENT WELL, I TRIED TO DUPLICATE AS MANY OF ITS CONDITIONS AS POSSIBLE. AND IF IT DIDN'T, I MADE SMALL ADJUSTMENTS TO MY REGIMEN.

IT'S TUESDAY... DON'T WEAR A SCOTS BRAND T-SHIRT.

LIFE HAD BECOME A LABORIOUS ROUND OF CHORES.

AT THE END OF THE DAY, IF I UNDRESSED IN THE WRONG ORDER, I HAD TO PUT MY CLOTHES BACK ON AND START AGAIN.

(AFTER I CLEARED IT AWAY, THE INVISIBLE SUBSTANCE WOULD IMMEDIATELY REPLENISH ITSELF.)

(THIRD TIME)

IT TOOK SEVERAL PAINSTAKING MINUTES TO LINE UP MY SHOES EXACTLY, SO AS TO SHOW NEITHER ONE PREFERENCE.

(THE LEFT ONE WAS MY FATHER.)

(THE RIGHT ONE WAS MY MOTHER.)

NO MATTER HOW TIRED I WAS AFTER ALL THIS, I HAD TO KISS EACH OF MY STUFFED ANIMALS--AND NOT JUST IN A PERFUNCTORY WAY. THEN I'D BRING ONE OF THE THREE BEARS TO BED WITH ME, ALTERNATING NIGHTLY BETWEEN MOTHER, FATHER, AND BABY.

THOUGH IT VERGES ON THE BATHETIC, I SHOULD POINT OUT THAT NO ONE HAD KISSED ME GOOD NIGHT IN YEARS.

ONCE MY MOTHER EXPRESSED CONCERN ABOUT MY BEHAVIOR.

ALISON, MAYBE YOU FEEL GUILTY ABOUT SOMETHING.

HAVE YOU HAD BAD THOUGHTS ABOUT ME OR DAD?

NO.

HAVE I?

I KNEW SHE'D GOTTEN THIS FROM DR. SPOCK. I HAD SPENT MANY AN HOUR BROWSING IN THAT EDIFYING VOLUME.

THE SECTION ON COMPULSIONS CAME CLOSEST TO DESCRIBING MY SYMPTOMS.

PROJECTILE **VOMITING?**

(MOM KEPT IT IN A DRAWER NEXT TO HER CHAIR.)

UNDESCENDED **TESTICLES?**

DAD'S HOME.

SO CLOSE, IN FACT, THAT I WONDER IF PERHAPS THAT'S WHERE I PICKED THEM UP.

FROM SIX TO ELEVEN

feeling that you ought to. It's what a psychiatrist calls a compulsion. Other examples are touching every third picket in a fence, making numbers come out even in some way, saying certain words before going through a door. If you think you have made a mistake, you must go way back to where you were absolutely sure that you were right, and start over again.

Everyone has hostile feelings at times toward the people who are close to him, but his conscience would

THE EXPLANATION OF REPRESSED HOSTILITY MADE NO SENSE TO ME. I CONTINUED READING, SEARCHING FOR SOMETHING MORE CONCRETE.

WHERE HAVE YOU **BEEN?** WE ATE TWO HOURS AGO!

I LEARNED ABOUT TICS, AND SOMETHING CALLED ST. VITUS' DANCE.

BUT THESE NERVOUS HABITS AND INVOLUNTARY TWITCHES WERE CHILD'S PLAY TO THE DARK FEAR OF ANNIHIL- ATION THAT MOTIVATED MY OWN RITUALS.

DON'T WALK AWAY FROM ME!

FOR CRISSAKES! I STOPPED FOR A HOT DOG!

STILL, I LIKED DR. SPOCK. READING HIM WAS A CURIOUS EXPERIENCE IN WHICH I WAS BOTH SUBJECT AND OBJECT, MY OWN PARENT AND MY OWN CHILD.

GOOD. I FLUSHED YOUR SUPPER DOWN THE TOILET.

IT WAS A SELF-SOOTHING, AUTISTIC LOOP.

AND INDEED, IF OUR FAMILY WAS A SORT OF ARTISTS' COLONY, COULD IT NOT BE EVEN MORE ACCURATELY DESCRIBED AS A MILDLY AUTISTIC COLONY?

OUR SELVES WERE ALL WE HAD.

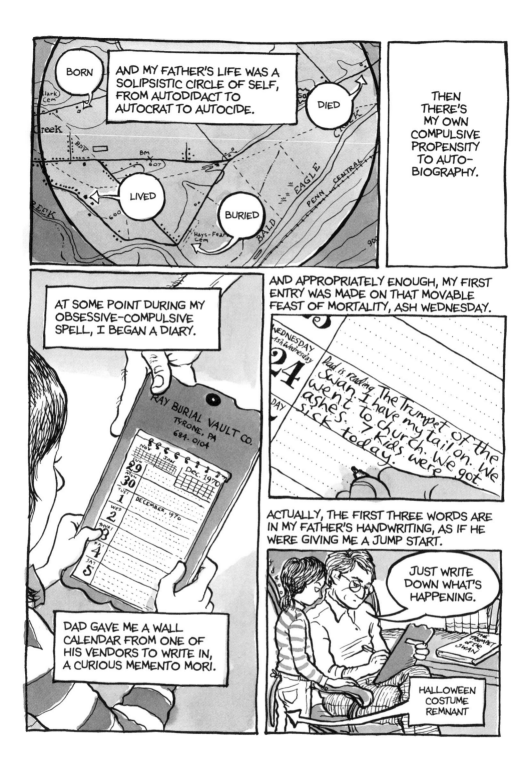

BORN

DIED

LIVED

BURIED

AND MY FATHER'S LIFE WAS A SOLIPSISTIC CIRCLE OF SELF, FROM AUTODIDACT TO AUTOCRAT TO AUTOCIDE.

THEN THERE'S MY OWN COMPULSIVE PROPENSITY TO AUTO-BIOGRAPHY.

AT SOME POINT DURING MY OBSESSIVE-COMPULSIVE SPELL, I BEGAN A DIARY.

RAY BURIAL VAULT CO.
TYRONE, PA
684-0104

DAD GAVE ME A WALL CALENDAR FROM ONE OF HIS VENDORS TO WRITE IN, A CURIOUS MEMENTO MORI.

AND APPROPRIATELY ENOUGH, MY FIRST ENTRY WAS MADE ON THAT MOVABLE FEAST OF MORTALITY, ASH WEDNESDAY.

Dad is reading The Trumpet of the Swan. I have my tail on. We went to church. We got ashes. 7 Kids were sick today.

ACTUALLY, THE FIRST THREE WORDS ARE IN MY FATHER'S HANDWRITING, AS IF HE WERE GIVING ME A JUMP START.

JUST WRITE DOWN WHAT'S HAPPENING.

HALLOWEEN COSTUME REMNANT

THE ENTRIES PROCEED BLANDLY ENOUGH. SOON I SWITCHED TO A DATE BOOK FROM AN INSURANCE AGENCY, WHICH AFFORDED MORE SPACE.

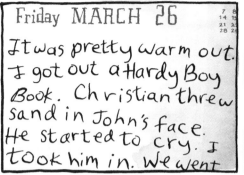

Friday MARCH 26

7 8
14 1
21 2
28 2

It was pretty warm out. I got out a Hardy Boy Book. Christian threw sand in John's face. He started to cry. I took him in. We went

BUT IN APRIL, THE MINUTELY-LETTERED PHRASE *I THINK* BEGINS TO CROP UP BETWEEN MY COMMENTS.

I finished ᴵᵀʰⁱⁿᵏ "The Cabin Island Mystery." Dad ordered 10 reams of paper! ᴵ ᵀʰⁱⁿᵏ We watched The Brady Bunch. I made popcorn. ᴵ ᵀʰⁱⁿᵏ There is popcorn left over

IT WAS A SORT OF EPISTEMOLOGICAL CRISIS. HOW DID I KNOW THAT THE THINGS I WAS WRITING WERE ABSOLUTELY, OBJECTIVELY TRUE?

ALL I COULD SPEAK FOR WAS MY OWN PERCEPTIONS, AND PERHAPS NOT EVEN THOSE.

MY SIMPLE, DECLARATIVE SENTENCES BEGAN TO STRIKE ME AS HUBRISTIC AT BEST, UTTER LIES AT WORST.

THE MOST STURDY NOUNS FADED TO FAINT APPROXIMATIONS UNDER MY PEN.

MY *I THINKS* WERE GOSSAMER SUTURES IN THAT GAPING RIFT BETWEEN SIGNIFIER AND SIGNIFIED. TO FORTIFY THEM, I PERSEVERATED UNTIL THEY WERE BLOTS.

Thursday MAY 6

9 Steve N. broke his arm
10 Steve C. cut his leg with
11 a Machete knife at camp. He
12 fainted! Mothe[r]
1 her hair done. I [got]
a page of math. Dad helped me.

MY DIARY WAS RAPIDLY BECOMING AS ONEROUS AS THE REST OF MY LIFE.

MY MOTHER APPARENTLY DECIDED THAT GIVING ME SOME ATTENTION MIGHT HELP, AND BEGAN READING TO ME WHILE I HAD MY BATH. BUT IT WAS TOO MUCH, TOO LATE.

...113, 114, 115, 116...

...FOR OF WHAT USE TO ANYONE WAS A CRIPPLE-HANDED SILVERSMITH?

DRIP DRIBBLE DRIP

JOHNNY TREMAIN

I WAS SO CONSUMED WITH ANXIETY THAT SHE WOULD STOP, THAT I COULDN'T ENJOY IT.

MATTERS WORSENED IN MY DIARY. TO SAVE TIME I CREATED A SHORTHAND VERSION OF *I THINK*, A CURVY CIRCUMFLEX.

SCHOOL. Tammi came down. ʌ We played casket with an old box. ʌ Dad wanted me to sweep the patio. ʌ He said I

SOON I BEGAN DRAWING IT RIGHT OVER NAMES AND PRONOUNS. IT BECAME A SORT OF AMULET, WARDING OFF EVIL FROM MY SUBJECTS.

Sun. JUNE 13

~~Mother~~ + ~~I~~ went to church. ~~Molly~~ came home with ~~us~~. ~~We~~ went swimming. ~~Dad~~ + ~~I~~ brought up the cushions for the

142

THEN I REALIZED I COULD DRAW THE SYMBOL OVER AN ENTIRE ENTRY.

THINGS WERE GETTING FAIRLY ILLEGIBLE BY AUGUST, WHEN WE HAD OUR CAMPING TRIP/INITIATION RITE AT THE BULLPEN.

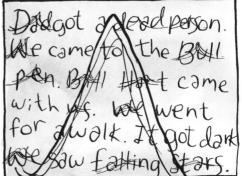

CONSIDERING THE PROFOUND PSYCHIC IMPACT OF THAT ADVENTURE, MY NOTES ON IT ARE SURPRISINGLY CURSORY. NO MENTION OF THE PIN-UP GIRL, THE STRIP MINE, OR BILL'S .22. JUST THE SNAKE--AND EVEN THAT WITH AN EXTREME ECONOMY OF STYLE.

AGAIN, THE TROUBLING GAP BETWEEN WORD AND MEANING. MY FEEBLE LANGUAGE SKILLS COULD NOT BEAR THE WEIGHT OF SUCH A LADEN EXPERIENCE.

143

IN A SIMILAR KIND OF LANGUAGE FAILURE, IN THE LOCAL DIALECT THE BULLPEN WAS SAID TO BE SITUATED SIMPLY "OUT ON THE MOUNTAIN," THAT IS, ON THE PLATEAU. IN THE PRIMEVAL WILDERNESS BEYOND THE FRONT, SPECIFICITY IS ABANDONED.

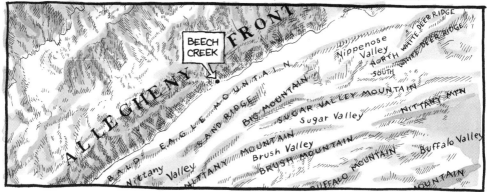

AND HURTLING TOWARD NEW YORK CITY ON ROUTE 80, SPEED AND PAVEMENT ERASED NOT JUST THE NAMES OF THINGS, BUT THE PARTICULAR, INTIMATE CONTOURS OF THE LANDSCAPE ITSELF.

IN THE END, ALTHOUGH THE ANONYMITY OF A CITY MIGHT HAVE SAVED MY FATHER'S LIFE, I CAN'T REALLY IMAGINE HIM ANYWHERE BUT BEECH CREEK.

LISTENING TO THE MUSEUM-TOUR TAPE, I'M SURPRISED BY HIS THICK PENNSYLVANIA ACCENT. DESPITE THE REFINED SUBJECT MATTER, HE SOUNDS BUMPKINISH.

IN THE BACK DISPLAY ROOM IS A FINE, CHERRY HEPPLEWHITE CORNER CUPBOARD OF ABOUT 1790. THIS WAS DONATED BY THE KLECKNER FAMILY OF SUGAR VALLEY. ON THE WALL ARE KITCHEN TOOLS USED BY EARLY FARM FAMILIES IN THE NINETEENTH CENTURY.

I HADN'T REMEMBERED THIS ABOUT HIM. BY THE TIME HE DIED, I HAD NEARLY SUCCEEDED IN SCRUBBING THOSE ELONGATED VOWELS FROM MY OWN SPEECH.

WHO'S THAT FROM?

MY DAD.

MY DERACINATION WAS KINDLY ABETTED BY VARIOUS FRIENDS AT COLLEGE.

YOUR DAY-UD?!

MY DAAAD, OKAY? MY **DAAAHD**.

BUT MY FATHER WAS PLANTED DEEP.

WHEN HE WAS IN THE ARMY AND DATING MY MOTHER, HE MADE PLANS FOR HER TO VISIT HIM AT HIS PARENT'S HOUSE ON AN UPCOMING LEAVE.

I have things to do at home. A dogwood to put in the front lawn. Sawdust to put around the foundation planting. I want to work in the earth. There are places I will show you. The farm, the jungle, the old canal. Do you understand?

IN AN EARLIER LETTER TO HER, HE DESCRIBES A WINTER SCENE.

Yesterday we skated on Beech Creek for miles through the silvery grey woods. How can I explain the creek? there are holes and crusty spots and solid mirrorlike passageways. It's dark bluish green under the iron bridge. Then on down between the island and the locks of the old canal the ice is like crystal and pale green weeds wave back and forth over blue rocks.

IN OUR *WIND IN THE WILLOWS* COLORING BOOK, MY FAVORITE PAGE WAS THE MAP.

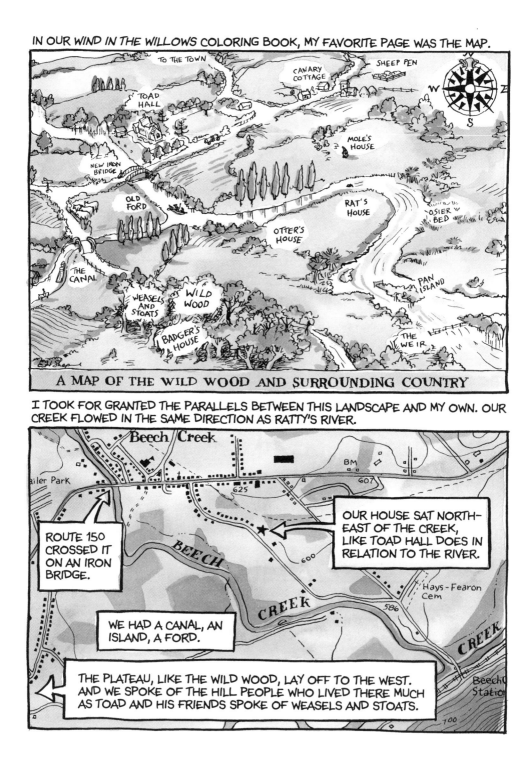

A MAP OF THE WILD WOOD AND SURROUNDING COUNTRY

I TOOK FOR GRANTED THE PARALLELS BETWEEN THIS LANDSCAPE AND MY OWN. OUR CREEK FLOWED IN THE SAME DIRECTION AS RATTY'S RIVER.

ROUTE 150 CROSSED IT ON AN IRON BRIDGE.

OUR HOUSE SAT NORTH-EAST OF THE CREEK, LIKE TOAD HALL DOES IN RELATION TO THE RIVER.

WE HAD A CANAL, AN ISLAND, A FORD.

THE PLATEAU, LIKE THE WILD WOOD, LAY OFF TO THE WEST. AND WE SPOKE OF THE HILL PEOPLE WHO LIVED THERE MUCH AS TOAD AND HIS FRIENDS SPOKE OF WEASELS AND STOATS.

BUT THE BEST THING ABOUT THE *WIND IN THE WILLOWS* MAP WAS ITS MYSTICAL BRIDGING OF THE SYMBOLIC AND THE REAL, OF THE LABEL AND THE THING ITSELF. IT WAS A CHART, BUT ALSO A VIVID, ALMOST ANIMATED PICTURE. LOOK CLOSELY...

...AND THERE'S MR. TOAD SPEEDING ALONG IN THE CAR HE BOUGHT AFTER BECOMING DISENCHANTED WITH HIS CANARY-COLORED CARAVAN.

IN SEPTEMBER OF MY OBSESSIVE-COMPULSIVE YEAR, THERE WAS A TERRIBLE ACCIDENT ON ROUTE 150.

THREE PEOPLE WERE KILLED IN A CRASH ABOUT TWO MILES BEYOND THE SPOT WHERE DAD WOULD DIE NINE YEARS LATER.

WE'D NEVER HAD A TRIPLE HEADER AT THE FUN HOME BEFORE.

BECHDEL FUNERAL HOME.

ONE OF THE VICTIMS WAS A DISTANT COUSIN OF MINE, A BOY EXACTLY MY AGE.

DAD EXPLAINED THAT HE HAD DIED FROM A BROKEN NECK.

HIS SKIN WAS GRAY, WHICH GAVE HIS BRIGHT BLOND CREWCUT THE EFFECT OF YELLOW TINT ON A BLACK-AND-WHITE PHOTOGRAPH.

MY DIARY ENTRIES FOR THAT WEEKEND ARE ALMOST COMPLETELY OBSCURED.

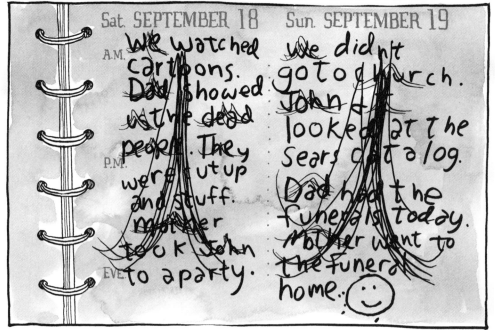

Sat. SEPTEMBER 18   Sun. SEPTEMBER 19

A.M. We watched cartoons. Dad showed us the dead people. They were cut up and stuff. Mother took John to a party.

We didn't go to church. John & I looked at the Sears catalog. Dad had the funerals today. Mother went to the funeral home. ☺

ON MONDAY MY BELABORED HAND IS INTERRUPTED BY MY MOTHER'S TIDY ONE.

Monday SEPTEMBER 20
Jewish New Year

We got up late.
I got a cold. We had art. We're doing repoussé with copper. Mother brought my math book to school. Becky's snake got out! We watched Laugh-In. I

FOR THE NEXT TWO MONTHS SHE TOOK DICTATION FROM ME, UNTIL MY "PENMANSHIP" IMPROVED.

THERE WAS A FIRE DRILL AND WE GOT FUDGESICLES. UH...I WASHED MY HAIR.

AND SLOWLY, I DID IMPROVE. ON MY WALL CALENDAR, I SET MYSELF DEADLINES BY WHICH TO ABANDON SPECIFIC COMPULSIONS, ONE AT A TIME.

| 3 Do english workbook out of order | 4 Stop folding towels funny. | 5 Get out Dad's side of car. | 6 Don't worry. You're safe. | 7 Toss shoes | 8 |
| 10 | 11 Wear "Scots" t-shirt | 12 | I INTERSPERSED THESE WITH SMALL ENCOURAGEMENTS. | | |

MY RECOVERY WAS HARDLY A JOYOUS EMBRACE OF LIFE'S ATTENDANT CHAOS--I WAS AS OBSESSIVE IN GIVING UP THE BEHAVIORS AS I HAD BEEN IN PURSUING THEM.

BUT I FELT A DEFINITE SENSE OF RELIEF, EVEN IF IT ONLY BARELY OUTSTRIPPED MY LINGERING ANXIETY.

149

MY FATHER ONCE NEARLY CAME TO BLOWS WITH A FEMALE DINNER GUEST ABOUT WHETHER A PARTICULAR PATCH OF EMBROIDERY WAS FUCHSIA OR MAGENTA.

BUT THE INFINITE GRADATIONS OF COLOR IN A FINE SUNSET--FROM SALMON TO CANARY TO MIDNIGHT BLUE--LEFT HIM WORDLESS.

CHAPTER 6

THE IDEAL HUSBAND

THE SUMMER I WAS THIRTEEN, MY FATHER'S SECRET ALMOST SURFACED.

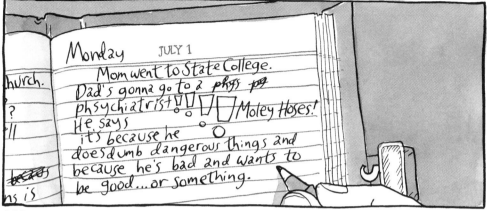

AT BREAKFAST THAT MORNING HE'D BEEN IN A JACKET AND TIE, NOT HIS USUAL VACATION DISHABILLE OF CUT-OFF JEANS.

THE IMPORT OF WHAT HE SAID WAS REMARKABLE, BUT LESS SO THAN THE FACT THAT HE WAS SAYING IT TO ME.

THE SUDDEN APPROXIMATION OF MY DULL, PROVINCIAL LIFE TO A *NEW YORKER* CARTOON WAS EXHILARATING.

BUT MY FATHER'S ABJECT AND SHAMEFUL MIEN QUICKLY SOBERED ME UP.

THERE WAS A LOT GOING ON THAT SUMMER. I'M GLAD I WAS TAKING NOTES.

OTHERWISE I'D FIND THE DEGREE OF SYNCHRONICITY IMPLAUSIBLE.

MY MOTHER WAS PLAYING LADY BRACKNELL IN A LOCAL PRODUCTION OF *THE IMPORTANCE OF BEING EARNEST.*

I AM ENGAGED TO MR. WORTHING, MAMA.

PARDON ME, YOU ARE NOT ENGAGED TO ANYONE.

WATERGATE WAS COMING TO A HEAD.

I GOT MY FIRST PERIOD.

WHEN YOU DO BECOME ENGAGED, I, OR YOUR FATHER, SHOULD HIS HEALTH PERMIT HIM, WILL INFORM YOU OF THE FACT.

AN ENGAGEMENT SHOULD COME ON A YOUNG GIRL AS A SURPRISE.

THIS JUXTAPOSITION OF THE LAST DAYS OF CHILDHOOD WITH THOSE OF NIXON AND THE END OF THAT LARGER, NATIONAL INNOCENCE MAY SEEM TRITE. BUT IT WAS ONLY ONE OF MANY HEAVY-HANDED PLOT DEVICES TO BEFALL MY FAMILY DURING THOSE STRANGE, HOT MONTHS.

IT IS HARDLY A MATTER THAT SHE COULD BE ALLOWED TO ARRANGE FOR HERSELF.

YOU LEFT OUT A PART. IT'S "AN ENGAGEMENT SHOULD COME ON A YOUNG GIRL AS A SURPRISE, PLEASANT OR UNPLEASANT AS THE CASE MAY BE."

IT'S SAID THAT HOMES WITH PUBESCENT CHILDREN IN THEM ARE MORE PRONE TO POLTERGEISTS--SPIRITS WHO TAKE PLEASURE IN CREATING DISORDER.

FIRST CAME THE PLAGUE OF LOCUSTS.

WHETHER OR NOT MY HORMONAL FLUCTUATIONS WERE ITS CAUSE, CHAOS WAS MOST ASSUREDLY AFOOT IN OUR HOUSEHOLD THAT SUMMER.

THEY LIVE UNDERGROUND FOR ALL THOSE YEARS, THEN SUDDENLY DECIDE TO CRAWL OUT? HOW DO THEY KNOW IT'S TIME?

THE EXPRESS
17-YEAR LOCUSTS RETURN TO AREA
GRAND JURY CITES NIXON AS UNINDIC CO-CONSPIRAT

MESSERSCHMITT
BF 109 G·10

APPARENTLY THE INSECTS SPENT THEIR YEARS UNDERGROUND IN A STATE OF PROTRACTED IMMATURITY.

WHEN IT WAS TIME TO BREED, THEY CRAWLED EN MASSE TO THE SURFACE, SHED THE SKINS OF THEIR NYMPH-HOOD, AND EMERGED AS WINGED ADULTS.

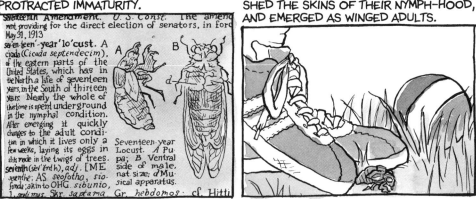

BY THE END OF THE FIRST WEEK IN JUNE, THE YARD WAS LITTERED WITH THEIR DISCARDED EXOSKELETONS.

NEXT THE LOCUSTS SETTLED DOWN TO AN ORGY IN OUR TALL MAPLE TREES, CLOAKING US FROM DAWN TO DUSK IN THE AMBIENT NOISE OF THEIR CONJUGAL EXERTIONS.

PERHAPS THEIR VIBRATING CHORUS SHOOK LOOSE THE SCREWS ON SOME COLLECTIVE LIBIDINAL IMPULSE, UNLEASHING IT INTO THE ATMOSPHERE.

AFTER A WEEK OR TWO, FINISHED WITH PASSING SPERM AND LAYING EGGS, THE LOCUSTS--MORE PROPERLY KNOWN AS PERIODIC CICADAS--SHUFFLED OFF THIS MORTAL COIL.

SOUNDS LIKE THEY'RE GETTING QUIETER.

LET'S PLAY THE TAPE AND COMPARE.

THAT'S WHEN I GOT MY PERIOD, TOWARD THE END OF JUNE. I DIDN'T TELL MY MOTHER.

NOW TO MINOR MATTERS. ARE YOUR PARENTS LIVING?

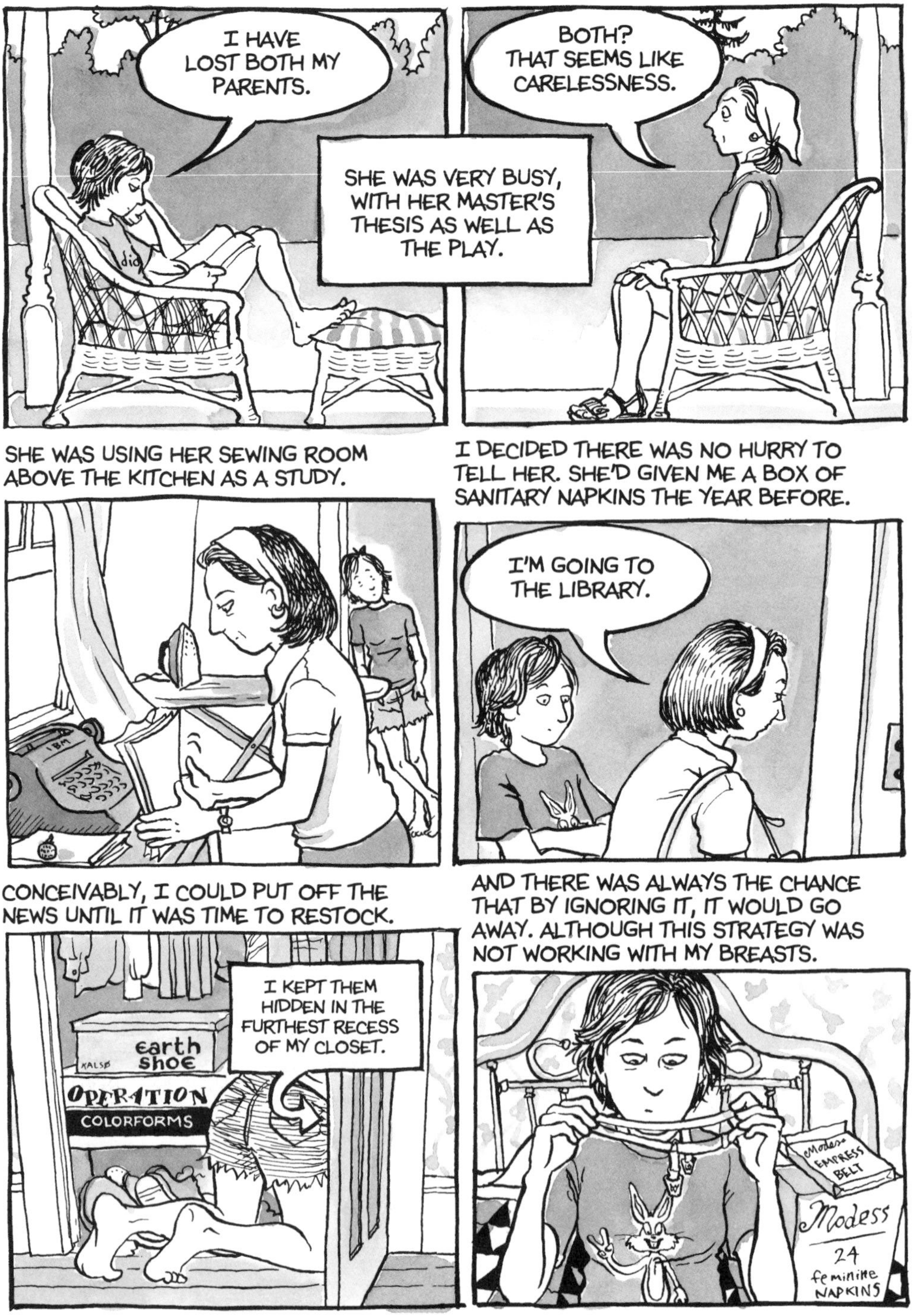
I HAVE LOST BOTH MY PARENTS.
BOTH? THAT SEEMS LIKE CARELESSNESS.
SHE WAS VERY BUSY, WITH HER MASTER'S THESIS AS WELL AS THE PLAY.
did
SHE WAS USING HER SEWING ROOM ABOVE THE KITCHEN AS A STUDY.
IBM
I DECIDED THERE WAS NO HURRY TO TELL HER. SHE'D GIVEN ME A BOX OF SANITARY NAPKINS THE YEAR BEFORE.
I'M GOING TO THE LIBRARY.
CONCEIVABLY, I COULD PUT OFF THE NEWS UNTIL IT WAS TIME TO RESTOCK.
I KEPT THEM HIDDEN IN THE FURTHEST RECESS OF MY CLOSET.
KALSØ
earth shoe
OPERATION
COLORFORMS
AND THERE WAS ALWAYS THE CHANCE THAT BY IGNORING IT, IT WOULD GO AWAY. ALTHOUGH THIS STRATEGY WAS NOT WORKING WITH MY BREASTS.
Modess EMPRESS BELT
Modess
24
feminine
NAPKINS

IT WAS JUST A SLIGHT, BROWNISH SECRETION. IT CERTAINLY DIDN'T REQUIRE ONE OF THE MAMMOTH NAPKINS, OR THE PORNOGRAPHIC BELT. A WAD OF TOILET PAPER SUFFICED.

IT WENT AWAY AFTER A FEW DAYS AND PASSED UNMENTIONED IN MY DIARY.

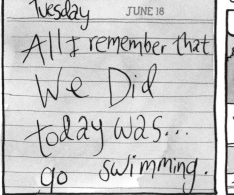

ABOUT THAT TIME, ON A WEDNESDAY AFTER-NOON, MY BEST FRIEND BETH'S FATHER AND STEPMOTHER SHOWED UP.

MY MOTHER WAS TAKEN ABACK BY THEIR GRAND GESTURE, BUT AGREED TO LET US GO.

THE GRYGLEWICZES LIVED IN TOWN, ON THE EDGE OF THE COLLEGE CAMPUS WHERE BETH'S FATHER AND STEPMOTHER TAUGHT.

IT WAS HARD TO REMEMBER TO ADDRESS BOTH PARENTS AS "DR. GRYGLEWICZ."

THANK YOU, MRS.... I MEAN...

WHAT IS THIS? PAELLA?

OUR VISIT WAS A VERITABLE SATURNALIA, A TWO-DAY BINGE OF NONSTOP PLAY.

SCOTT, GIMME "A CHILD'S GARDEN OF VERSES."

BLAST!

COVER ME. I'M GOING IN.

AND "DR. JEKYLL AND MR. HYDE," THANK YOU VERY MUCH.

GAME OF "AUTHORS"

POLICE! FREEZE!

ONE OF DR. GRYGLE-WICZ'S MANY INTER-ESTING PAINTINGS OF DR. GRYGLEWICZ.

SPREAD 'EM, PUNKS!

160

IT NEVER OCCURRED TO ME TO WONDER WHAT MY FATHER HAD BEEN UP TO DURING OUR ABSENCE. BUT AS IT HAPPENED, HE'D BEEN ON A SPREE OF HIS OWN.

ON THURSDAY AT DUSK, HE'D DRIVEN OVER TO THE NEXT VALLEY. I KNOW THIS BECAUSE I LOOKED IT UP IN THE POLICE REPORT TWENTY-SEVEN YEARS LATER.

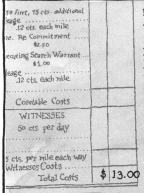

Mark Douglas Walsh, Booneville, Penna., witness for the Commonwealth, testified under oath that on June 20, 1974, between the hours of 9PM and 10PM he saw Bruce Allen Bechdel, with whom he was acquainted. Mr. Bechdel asked him where his brother David was and that he got in the car with Mr. Bechdel and they went to look for his brother. During the course of the evening, defendant purchased a six-pack of beer. Witness stated that Mr. Bechdel offered him a beer and he took it and drank it. Mr. Bechdel asked him what he did and what his brother was doing at that time. He then let him off in the vicinity of his home. Witness testified that at the time of this incident he was seventeen years old and that he told Mr. Bechdel his age.

THEY NEVER DID FIND MARK'S OLDER BROTHER, DAVE.

HE'D BEEN AT HOME ALL NIGHT, AND WHEN DAD DROPPED MARK OFF, DAVE RECOGNIZED THE CAR AND CALLED THE COPS.

I DON'T KNOW WHEN THE SUMMONS ARRIVED. NO TROOPER CAME TO OUR DOOR, AND THERE'S NO CLUE IN MY DIARY THAT ANYTHING WAS AMISS DURING THE FOLLOWING WEEK.

Thursday   JUNE 27

Scott G. came up. He and Chris played in their spy club. I pretended I was a rich guy, a police officer, and a tennis player, and went to their office with cases for them to solve.
Then we put on clown make-up and sat out front. We wanted to scare cars, only... ONLY...

BUT THEN, MY DIARY WAS NO LONGER THE UTTERLY RELIABLE DOCUMENT IT HAD BEEN IN MY YOUTH. A FALTERING, ELLIPTIC TONE WAS CREEPING IN.

scare cars, only... we wanted Tammi drove by. Holy snot! She called me later and told me how odd? (idiotic) we looked. Uh... Ma & Pa went to the Playhouse to see "No Sex, please... We're British." They liked it... I guess.

INDEED, ACTUAL ELLIPSES BEGAN RIDDLING THE PAGES--THOUGH I USED THOSE THREE DOTS TO INDICATE NOT SO MUCH OMISSION AS HESITATION.

ON THE FIRST OF JULY, DAD AND I HAD OUR ENCOUNTER IN THE KITCHEN.

WHERE ARE YOU GOING?

TO DANVILLE.

TO THE MENTAL HOSPITAL?

I...I HAVE TO SEE A PSYCHIATRIST.

PERHAPS THIS WAS A PRE-EMPTIVE STRATEGY RECOM-MENDED BY HIS LAWYER.

LATER THAT SAME DAY, MY MOTHER WENT TO SEE HER THESIS ADVISOR.

WHEN SHE GOT HOME THAT AFTERNOON, SHE WAS UPSET.

AFTER YOU DUST AND VACUUM, YOU CAN GO SWIMMING.

I CAN'T BELIEVE HE WANTS MORE REVISIONS!

IN EVEN THE MOST ROUTINE ACTIVITIES, MY MOTHER HELD TO EXACTING STANDARDS.

WHEN AM I SUPPOSED TO FIND THE TIME? REHEARSAL STARTS WEDNESDAY AND I DON'T HAVE MY LINES YET!

MOUSSAKA FOR FIVE AND FRESH SOURDOUGH BREAD IN FIFTEEN MINUTES

BUT BEING IN A PLAY CONSUMED HER UTTERLY. TERRIFIED OF GOING BLANK ONSTAGE, SHE LEARNED EVERYONE ELSE'S LINES ALONG WITH HER OWN.

JACK. BETWEEN SEVEN AND EIGHT THOUSAND A YEAR.

IN LAND, OR IN INVEST-MENTS?

SHE EVEN WORKED ON HER OWN COSTUMES.

JACK: IN INVEST-MENTS, CHIEFLY.

THAT IS SATISFACTORY.

WE KNEW BETTER THAN TO ASK WHEN OPENING NIGHT WAS. BUT WITH THIS PLAY, MOM'S USUAL ANXIETY LEVEL HAD INCREASED BY AN ORDER OF MAGNITUDE.

I **DON'T KNOW!** I DON'T WANT TO THINK ABOUT IT! AND DON'T TELL ME WHEN YOU'RE COMING. JUST SIT IN THE BACK, THAT'S ALL I ASK.

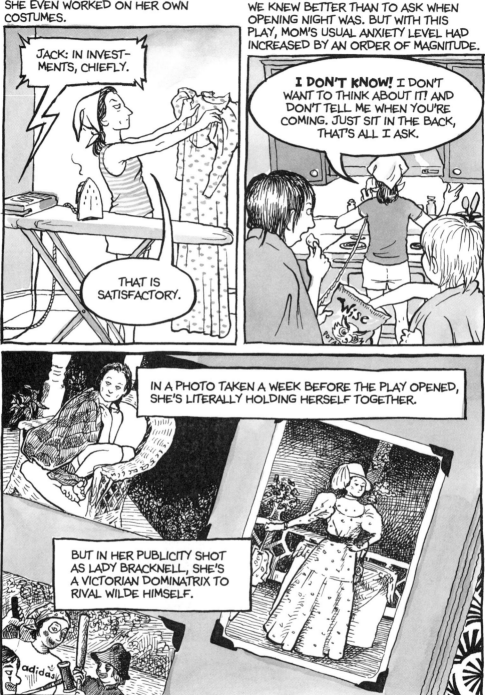

IN A PHOTO TAKEN A WEEK BEFORE THE PLAY OPENED, SHE'S LITERALLY HOLDING HERSELF TOGETHER.

BUT IN HER PUBLICITY SHOT AS LADY BRACKNELL, SHE'S A VICTORIAN DOMINATRIX TO RIVAL WILDE HIMSELF.

I LOVED SEEING HER IN CHARACTER AS THAT AUGUST MATRON. IN A FITTING COINCIDENCE, LADY BRACKNELL'S FIRST NAME, AUGUSTA, WAS MY MOTHER'S MIDDLE NAME.

I AM REALLY ONLY EIGHTEEN, BUT I ALWAYS ADMIT TO TWENTY WHEN I GO TO EVENING PARTIES.

YOU ARE QUITE RIGHT IN MAKING SOME SLIGHT ALTERATION. INDEED, NO WOMAN SHOULD EVER BE QUITE ACCURATE ABOUT HER AGE. IT LOOKS SO CALCULATING.

THIS WAS THE FIRST TIME I'D BEEN OLD ENOUGH TO HELP HER RUN LINES. SURPRISED THAT AN ADULT PLAY COULD BE SO FUNNY, I CONTINUED READING ON MY OWN.

SNRK.

MY ENJOYMENT WAS UNENCUMBERED BY ANY KNOWLEDGE OF WILDE'S MARTYROLOGY.

DAD! "I NEVER TRAVEL WITHOUT MY DIARY. ONE SHOULD ALWAYS HAVE SOMETHING SENSATIONAL TO READ ON THE TRAIN."

I TOOK THE PLAY AT FACE VALUE, AS PERHAPS QUEEN VICTORIA HAD.

I WAS QUITE RIGHT IN SAYING YOU WERE A BUNBURYIST. YOU ARE ONE OF THE MOST ADVANCED BUNBURYISTS I KNOW.

WHAT ON EARTH DO YOU MEAN?

THE COVERT REFERENCES TO HOMOSEXUALITY ELUDED ME.

YOU HAVE INVENTED A VERY USEFUL YOUNGER BROTHER CALLED ERNEST, IN ORDER THAT YOU MAY BE ABLE TO COME UP TO TOWN AS OFTEN AS YOU LIKE. I HAVE INVENTED...

WAIT, WAIT.

NOW I KNOW IT WAS RIGHT AFTER *THE IMPORTANCE* OPENED ON VALENTINE'S DAY, 1895, THAT WILDE'S TRIALS BEGAN.

HE'D JUST RETURNED FROM ALGIERS, WHERE HE AND ALFRED DOUGLAS HAD BEEN DISPORTING THEMSELVES WTIH THE LOCAL BOYS.

DOUGLAS'S FATHER DELIVERED HIS FAMOUS NOTE TO WILDE'S CLUB, ACCUSING HIM OF BEING A SODOMITE. INDIGNANT, WILDE TOOK HIM TO COURT FOR LIBEL AND LOST.

I WANT YOU DOWNSTAGE FOR THIS LINE. WE NEED TO MOVE THE CUCUMBER SANDWICHES.

IN *THE IMPORTANCE*, ILLICIT DESIRE IS ENCODED AS ONE CHARACTER'S UNCONTROLLABLE GLUTTONY.

PLEASE DON'T TOUCH THE CUCUMBER SANDWICHES. THEY ARE ORDERED SPECIALLY FOR AUNT AUGUSTA.

THEN WILDE WAS TRIED FOR COMMITTING INDECENT ACTS AND SENT TO PRISON WHILE BOTH *THE IMPORTANCE* AND *THE IDEAL HUSBAND* WERE PLAYING TO FULL HOUSES.

LET'S TAKE IT FROM "PLEASE DON'T TOUCH."

BUT YOU'VE BEEN EATING THEM ALL ALONG.

MOM HELPED THE PROP MISTRESS FIND A RECIPE FOR CUCUMBER SANDWICHES. WE ATE THEM ALL SUMMER.

ON THE AFTERNOON BEFORE OPENING NIGHT, THE DRS. GRYGLEWICZ, IN A SECOND GRAND GESTURE, DELIVERED A BREATHTAKING BUNCH OF LILIES.

DAD! YOU'RE EATING THEM FASTER THAN WE CAN MAKE THEM!

WILDE WOULD BRING ARMLOADS OF THESE TO THE ACTRESS LILLIE LANGTRY.

MOM WAS AGAIN TAKEN ABACK.

THEY'RE BEAUTIFUL. BUT I CAN'T TALK NOW. I'M GOING UPSTAIRS.

WE UNDERSTAND! THE DIVA MUST COMPOSE HERSELF!

HOW ABOUT A GIN AND TONIC? ALISON, MAKE SOME CUCUMBER SANDWICHES.

YEARS LATER I LEARNED THAT THE GRYGLEWICZES ONCE MADE A PROPOSITION, WHICH MY PARENTS DECLINED, THAT THE FOUR OF THEM ENGAGE IN GROUP SEX.

SHE GETS NERVOUS.

OF COURSE SHE DOES.

SHE'LL BE BRILLIANT. IT'S THE PERFECT ROLE FOR HER.

MOM *WAS* BRILLIANT. FROM HER FIRST ENTRANCE, SHE WAS IN COMPLETE COMMAND.

GOOD AFTERNOON, DEAR ALGERNON. I HOPE YOU ARE BEHAVING VERY WELL.

I'M FEELING VERY WELL, AUNT AUGUSTA.

THAT'S NOT QUITE THE SAME THING. IN FACT THE TWO THINGS RARELY GO TOGETHER.

THE PLAY RAN FOR A WEEK. ALL THE ACTORS EXCEPT MOM FLUFFED THEIR LINES AT LEAST ONCE.

ALL WOMEN BECOME LIKE THEIR MOTHERS. THAT IS THEIR TRAGEDY. NO MAN DOES. THAT'S HERS. **HIS**.

THE DAY AFTER THE PLAY CLOSED, REAL LIFE RESUMED WITH A VENGEANCE. MY SECRETION WAS BACK.

FACED NOW WITH INCONTROVERTIBLE EVIDENCE, I FELT OBLIGATED TO ENTER IT INTO THE RECORD.

WHEN I WAS TEN, I WAS OBSESSED WITH MAKING SURE MY DIARY ENTRIES BORE NO FALSE WITNESS.

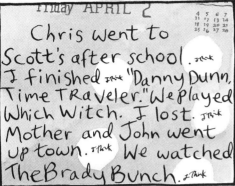

Friday APRIL 2

Chris went to Scott's after school. J.Think I finished J.Think "Danny Dunn, Time Traveler." We played Which Witch. I lost. J.Think Mother and John went up town. J.Think We watched The Brady Bunch. J.Think

BUT AS I AGED, HARD FACTS GAVE WAY TO VAGARIES OF EMOTION AND OPINION.

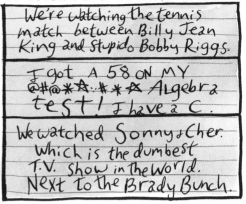

We're watching the tennis match between Billy Jean King and stupid Bobby Riggs.

I got A 58 ON MY @#@*#.#**# ALgebra test! I have a C.

We watched Sonny & Cher. Which is the dumbest T.V. show in the World. Next to the Brady Bunch.

FALSE HUMILITY, OVERWROUGHT PENMAN-SHIP, AND SELF-DISGUST BEGAN TO CLOUD MY TESTIMONY...

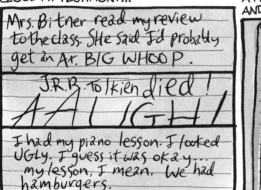

Mrs. Bitner read my review to the class. She said I'd probably get an A+. BIG WHOOP.

J.R.R. Tolkien died! AALIGHH!

I had my piano lesson. I looked UGLY. I guess it was okay... my lesson, I mean. We had hamburgers.

...UNTIL, IN THIS MOMENTOUS ENTRY, THE TRUTH IS BARELY PERCEPTIBLE BEHIND A HEDGE OF QUALIFIERS, ENCRYPTION, AND STRAY PUNCTUATION.

Wednesday   JULY 24

I think I started Ning or something. (HA HA)? HOW HORRID!

I ENCODED THE WORD MENSTRUATING ACCORDING TO THE PRACTICE I'D LEARNED IN ALGEBRA OF DENOTING COMPLEX OR UNKNOWN QUANTITIES WITH LETTERS.

"X" WOULD HAVE BEEN OBVIOUS. USING "N" CREATED A PARTICIPLE SO NONDESCRIPT IT COULD MEAN PRACTICALLY ANYTHING.

IN FACT, SO CERTAIN WAS I OF *NING'S* INDECIPHERABILITY THAT I USED IT THREE YEARS LATER TO CAMOUFLAGE AN ENTIRELY DIFFERENT BIOLOGICAL EVENT.

Sun. March 6 –
I gave up ning for lent and I just did it twice.
Argh!! I saw a neat play called 'Rhinoceros' at the college with Beth. Then we went to Mc Donald's &

IF ONLY I HAD READ WILDE'S *PICTURE OF DORIAN GRAY*, I MAY HAVE TAKEN SOME COMFORT IN THE KNOWLEDGE THAT "THE ONLY WAY TO GET RID OF A TEMPTATION IS TO YIELD TO IT."

ALTHOUGH I DID NOT ALLUDE TO MASTURBATION IN MY DIARY UNTIL I WAS SIXTEEN, I BEGAN THE ASSIDUOUS PRACTICE OF THAT ACTIVITY SOON AFTER I GOT MY FIRST PERIOD.

I DIDN'T KNOW THEN THAT THERE WAS A WORD FOR THE ODDLY GRATIFYING MOTION OF ROCKING BACK AND FORTH IN MY CHAIR AS I DREW AT MY DESK.

THE NEW REALIZATION THAT I COULD ILLUSTRATE MY OWN FANTASIES FILLED ME WITH AN OMNIPOTENCE THAT WAS IN ITSELF EROTIC.

IN THE FLAT CHESTS AND SLIM HIPS OF MY SURROGATES, I FOUND RELEASE FROM MY OWN INCREASING BURDEN OF FLESH.

NOR DID I KNOW THAT THERE WAS A WORD FOR THE INEVITABLE RESULT OF THIS SHIFTING ABOUT IN MY CHAIR...

...THE IMPLOSIVE SPASM SO STAGGER-INGLY COMPLETE AND PERFECT THAT FOR A FEW BRIEF MOMENTS I COULD NOT QUESTION ITS INHERENT MORAL VALIDITY.

WHEN I ACCIDENTALLY RAN ACROSS THIS WORD IN THE DICTIONARY ONE DAY, IT WAS INSTANTLY FAMILIAR, BEFORE I EVEN GOT TO THE DEFINITION.

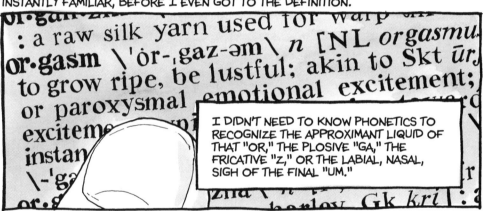

: a raw silk yarn used for warp

or·gasm \'ȯr-ˌgaz-əm\ n [NL orgasmu. to grow ripe, be lustful; akin to Skt ūr, or paroxysmal emotional excitement;

I DIDN'T NEED TO KNOW PHONETICS TO RECOGNIZE THE APPROXIMANT LIQUID OF THAT "OR," THE PLOSIVE "GA," THE FRICATIVE "Z," OR THE LABIAL, NASAL, SIGH OF THE FINAL "UM."

THE WORD ENTERED MY VOCABULARY, BUT NOT MY DIARY. A SIN OF OMISSION?

PERHAPS. BUT IF THE THING OMITTED WERE ITSELF A SIN, IT SEEMED TO ME (IN ANOTHER PRACTICAL USE OF ALGEBRA) THAT A CANCELING-OUT OCCURRED.

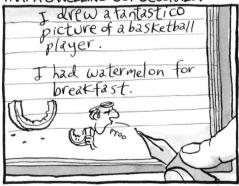

I drew a fantastico picture of a basketball player.

I had watermelon for breakfast.

PTOO

OR PERHAPS MY REASONING WAS MORE INFLUENCED BY SOCIAL STUDIES THAN MATH. GAPS, ERASURES, AND OTHER LACUNAE HAD SATURATED THE NEWS FOR THE PAST YEAR.

INTERESTINGLY, MY PERIOD ENTRY CONTINUES WITH A RARE MENTION OF THE POLITICAL CRISIS, WHICH HAD JUST REACHED A SIMILAR STAGE OF UNDENIABILITY.

THE ONLY OTHER REFERENCES IN MY DIARY TO THE SCANDAL ARE AN OFFHAND COMMENT EARLIER THAT YEAR...

Wednesday   JULY 24
I think I started Ning or something.
(HAHA)?
⋮ ⋮ HOW HORRID!
I made fudge. Uncle Joe came.
Uh... they're gonna make Nixon
hand over the tapes. Good, eh?

We watched   I got out "Little
Tricky Dick.   Women."
                     It's A Book.

...AND THE SANCTIMONIOUS OBSERVATION THE PREVIOUS SUMMER THAT...

George Washington never had
a Watergate. Think about it.

THE HEARINGS HAD BEEN MOSTLY A NUISANCE TO ME.

BUT NOW EVEN I BEGAN TO TAKE NOTICE AS THE TRUTH WORMED ITS WAY, LIKE A LARVAL CICADA, TOWARD DAYLIGHT.

AS THE MOMENTUM FOR IMPEACHMENT BUILT, SO DID OUR DOMESTIC TENSION.

I THOUGHT YOU ALREADY REVISED IT.

THE EXPRESS
IMPEACHMENT ADVOCATES WIN FIRST VOTE

I DID! HE'S STILL NOT SATISFIED! I HAVE TO REWRITE TWO ENTIRE CHAPTERS!

IT WAS ONE AFTERNOON AROUND THIS TIME THAT I FOUND MYSELF ALONE IN MY AUNT'S POOL WITH MY MOTHER. THE IDEAL OPPORTUNITY TO DELIVER MY NEWS.

"MOM, I THINK I STARTED GETTING MY..." **NO.** "MOM, I GOT MY..." **NO.** "HEY, MOM! GUESS WHAT!"

BUT AS IT HAPPENED, MOM HAD SOME NEWS OF HER OWN.

ALISON, THERE'S A CHANCE WE MIGHT HAVE TO MOVE.

WHAT?

DAD HAS TO GO TO COURT IN A FEW DAYS, AND HE MIGHT LOSE HIS JOB. HE BOUGHT A BEER FOR A BOY WHO WASN'T OLD ENOUGH.

WHERE WOULD WE GO?

MAYBE TO NEW YORK, OR MASSACHUSETTS, WHERE WE VISITED LAST SUMMER.

NEW ENGLAND PROMISED AN ALLURING COHERENCE--LIKE LIFE ON TV, OR IN THE MIRROR--THAT MY CURRENT EXISTENCE WAS SADLY LACKING.

IN MY DIARY THAT NIGHT, I REMARKED UPON THIS EXCHANGE WITH THE SAME PHRASE I HAD USED ABOUT MY PERIOD.

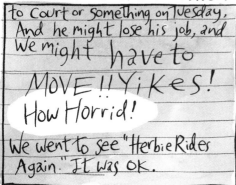

to court or something on Tuesday, And he might lose his job, and We might have to MOVE!! Yikes! How Horrid! We went to see "Herbie Rides Again." It was OK.

HOW HORRID HAS A SLIGHTLY FACETIOUS TONE THAT STRIKES ME AS WILDEAN.

IT APPEARS TO EMBRACE THE ACTUAL HORROR--PUBERTY, PUBLIC DIS-GRACE--THEN AT THE LAST SECOND NIMBLY SIDESTEPS IT, LAUGHING.

MY FATHER HAD SLIPPED SOMEWHAT IN MY ESTIMATION, BUT I WAS STILL SYMPA-THETIC TOWARD HIM.

THE REAL ACCUSATION DARED NOT SPEAK ITS NAME.

HIS LEGAL ENTANGLEMENT SEEMED LIKE A TECHNICALITY TO ME. BUT I DIDN'T KNOW THEN THAT "FURNISHING A MALT BEVERAGE TO A MINOR" WAS THE LEAST OF HIS TROUBLES.

I CAN ONLY SPECULATE ON THE EXACT NATURE OF HIS RELATIONS WITH THE BROTHERS IN THE NEXT VALLEY.

BUT IN THE END HE WAS EXPOSED BY ONE OF THEM--JUST LIKE OSCAR WILDE WAS CONDEMNED BY THE TESTIMONY OF HIS ROUGH TRADE.

ON THE DAY BEFORE MY MOTHER'S THESIS WAS DUE, A SUDDEN STORM WHIPPED UP. THIS WAS NOT UNUSUAL ON A SUMMER AFTERNOON, AND WE KNEW WHAT TO DO.

BATTEN THE HATCHES!

I'LL DO THE PORCH. GO SHUT ALL THE WEST WINDOWS.

I'LL GET THE CAR WINDOWS!

BUT THERE WAS SOMETHING UNUSUAL ABOUT THE WAY THE STIFF BREEZE INVERTED THE LEAVES OF THE SILVER MAPLES OUTSIDE MY BEDROOM.

THEIR PALE UNDERSIDES GLOWED IN THE ODD, GREEN LIGHT.

AS SOON AS I SHUT THE WINDOW, THE RAIN HIT IT LIKE A FIREHOSE.

THE WIND ROARED AND PELTED CHUNKS OF HAIL AGAINST THE HOUSE.

EMERGENCY! WOOOOOOO!

I WAS IN THE KITCHEN WHEN THE CEILING STARTED TO LEAK.

I'D FORGOTTEN THE SEWING ROOM WINDOW. IT WASN'T USUALLY OPEN, BUT MOM HAD BEEN TYPING IN THERE EARLIER.

MY PAPER!

WHEN THE STORM PASSED, WE VENTURED OUTSIDE. THE TEMPERATURE HAD DROPPED TWENTY DEGREES. A SOFT DRIZZLE FELL FROM THE HIGH, QUICK CLOUDS.

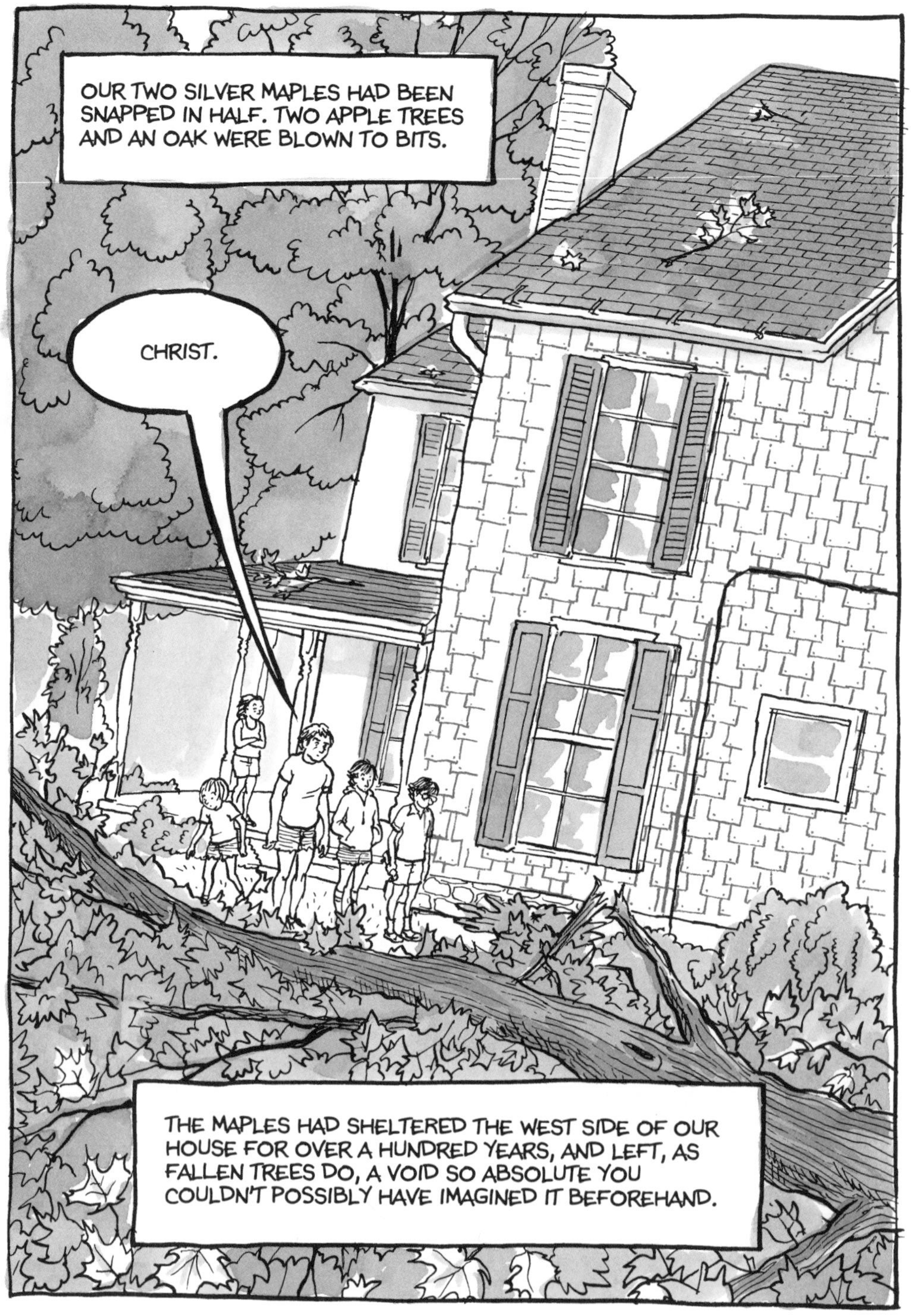
OUR TWO SILVER MAPLES HAD BEEN SNAPPED IN HALF. TWO APPLE TREES AND AN OAK WERE BLOWN TO BITS.
CHRIST.
THE MAPLES HAD SHELTERED THE WEST SIDE OF OUR HOUSE FOR OVER A HUNDRED YEARS, AND LEFT, AS FALLEN TREES DO, A VOID SO ABSOLUTE YOU COULDN'T POSSIBLY HAVE IMAGINED IT BEFOREHAND.

NONE OF THE NEIGHBORS HAD MUCH DAMAGE. IT WAS AS IF A TORNADO HAD TOUCHED DOWN PRECISELY AT OUR ADDRESS.

YET THE HOUSE ITSELF HAD ESCAPED HARM, AS HAD THE GARAGE AND CARS. EVEN THE CAT SAUNTERED HOME NOT JUST UNSCATHED, BUT DRY.

IN THIS LIGHT, THE RING OF DOWNED TREES CONVEYS A THEME LESS OF DESTRUCTION THAN OF NARROW ESCAPE.

MOM RETYPED HER THESIS THAT NIGHT.

IT PASSED MUSTER THE NEXT DAY.

MOM, COME SEE WHERE THE TREES WERE!

I NEED A MARTINI.

BUT ONE MORE NARROW ESCAPE WAS YET TO COME.

DAD'S HEARING WAS ON AUGUST 6TH. EACH OF THE BROTHERS TESTIFIED. THE MAGISTRATE STUCK STRICTLY TO THE LIQUOR CHARGE.

BUT A WHIFF OF THE SEXUAL AROMA OF THE TRUE OFFENSE COULD BE DETECTED IN THE SENTENCE.

HE WAS NOT HAULED OFF TO READING GAOL. WE DID NOT HAVE TO MOVE.

TWO DAYS AFTER DAD'S COURT DATE, NIXON THREW IN THE TOWEL.

TO LEAVE OFFICE BEFORE MY TERM IS COMPLETED IS ABHORRENT TO EVERY INSTINCT IN MY BODY.

AS SUMMER DREW TO AN END, A DISPIRITED NOTE ENTERED MY DIARY.

Saturday AUGUST 24

We went to the ford to work on our dam. But we quit, because we all decided it was too futile a task. We went to Tammi's to watch a movie, but it wasn't on, so we watched another show, which was a piece of crap. Then we played Cops & Robbers, which was stupid. Dad got another bureau for my room.

ON LABOR DAY, WE HOSTED A LAWN PARTY FOR THE PLAYHOUSE CAST AND CREW.

"JACK," FROM THE IMPORTANCE.

FORD
TIME
THE HEALING BEGINS

A FEW DAYS LATER I TURNED FOURTEEN.

THANKS, MOM!

GENTLEMEN'S QUARTERLY?

UH...I'M THINKING OF BEING A FASHION DESIGNER.

BETH GRYGLEWICZ WAS TRYING TO IMPROVE MY SOCIAL SKILLS.

HE'S CUTE.

I DON'T WANNA GO TO THE GAME. I HATE FOOTBALL.

181

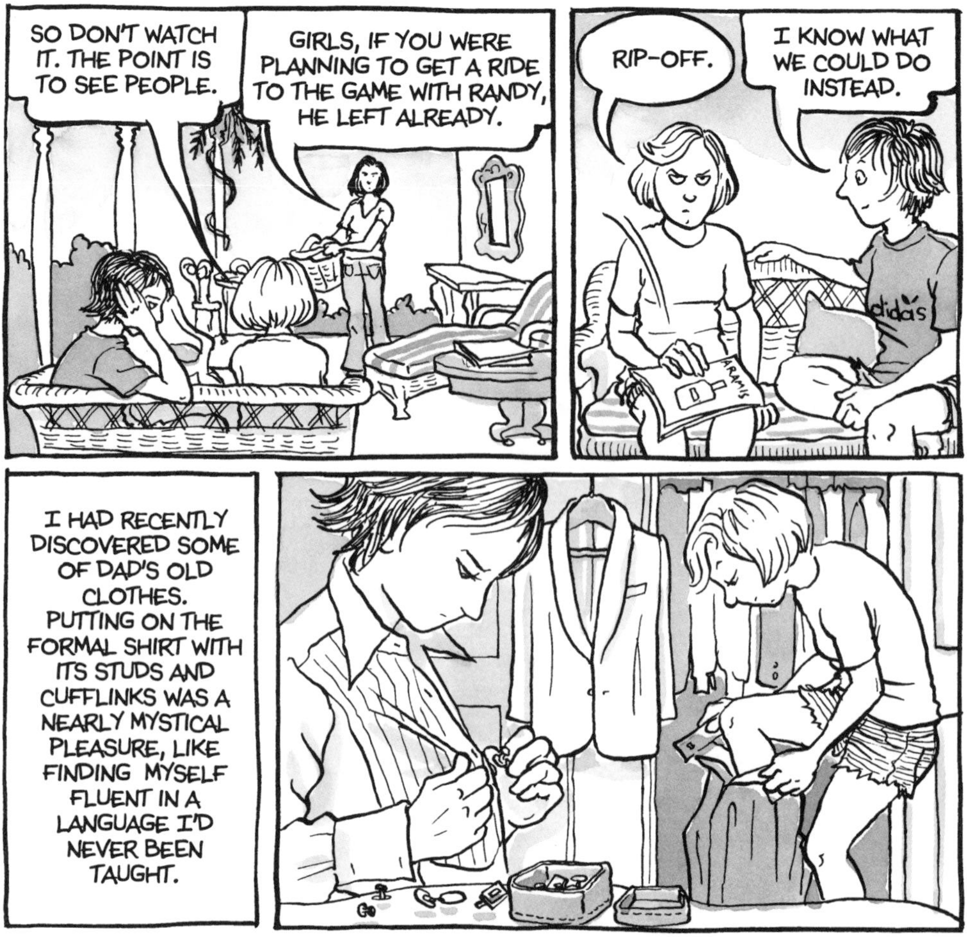
SO DON'T WATCH IT. THE POINT IS TO SEE PEOPLE.
GIRLS, IF YOU WERE PLANNING TO GET A RIDE TO THE GAME WITH RANDY, HE LEFT ALREADY.
RIP-OFF.
I KNOW WHAT WE COULD DO INSTEAD.
ARAMIS
I HAD RECENTLY DISCOVERED SOME OF DAD'S OLD CLOTHES. PUTTING ON THE FORMAL SHIRT WITH ITS STUDS AND CUFFLINKS WAS A NEARLY MYSTICAL PLEASURE, LIKE FINDING MYSELF FLUENT IN A LANGUAGE I'D NEVER BEEN TAUGHT.

IT FELT TOO GOOD TO ACTUALLY BE GOOD. BUT BETH WAS GOING ALONG WITH IT.

SO FAR, ANYWAY.

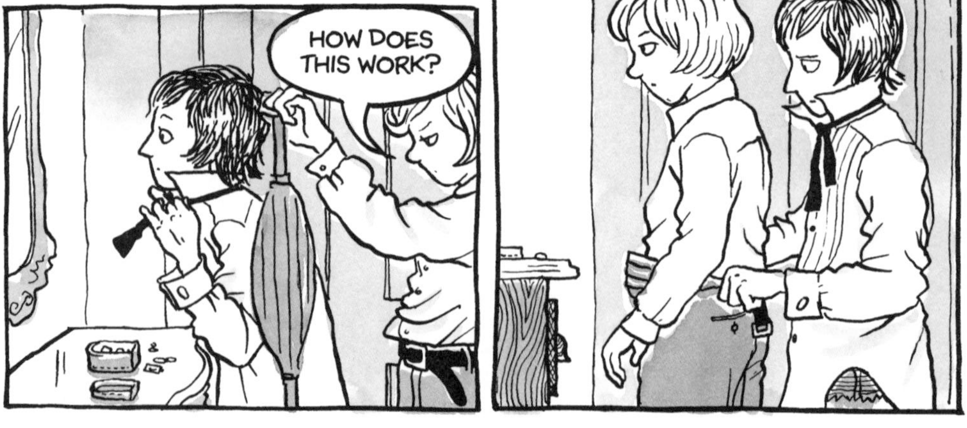
HOW DOES THIS WORK?

WE BEGAN FLESHING OUT A SCENARIO.

BILLY MCKEAN. FASTEST CON MAN IN THE EAST.

BOBBY MCCOOL.

EXCUSE ME, SIR. YOU LOOK LIKE YOU COULD USE SOME LIFE INSURANCE.

SIGN WITH US. NO MUSS, NO FUSS.

BUT WE COULDN'T SUSTAIN IT.

MAN, IT'S HOT. LET'S TAKE THIS STUFF OFF.

YEAH.

THAT NIGHT, I DESCRIBED THIS LAST MELANCHOLY FORAY INTO PLAY-ACTING.

Con men named Billy McKean + Bobby McCool. But then we quit because it was too hot to keep Dad's suits on, and we couldn't think of anything else to do. Our school won the football game. We could have gone to it, and the dance, but we stupidly missed our ride. John stayed over at Sean's.

MY PROFESSION OF DISAPPOINTMENT AT MISSING THE GAME AND THE DANCE WAS AN UTTER FALSEHOOD, OF COURSE.

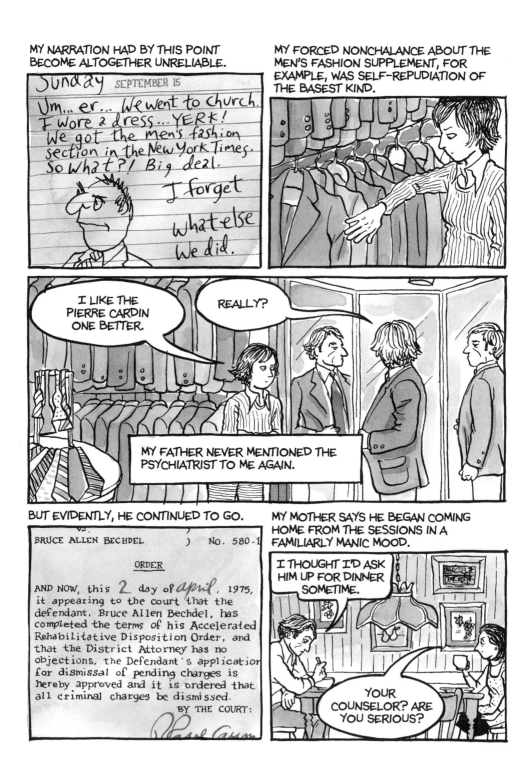

MY NARRATION HAD BY THIS POINT BECOME ALTOGETHER UNRELIABLE.

Sunday SEPTEMBER 15

Um... er... We went to church. I wore a dress... YERK! We got the men's fashion section in the New York Times. So what?! Big deal.

I forget what else we did.

MY FORCED NONCHALANCE ABOUT THE MEN'S FASHION SUPPLEMENT, FOR EXAMPLE, WAS SELF-REPUDIATION OF THE BASEST KIND.

I LIKE THE PIERRE CARDIN ONE BETTER.

REALLY?

MY FATHER NEVER MENTIONED THE PSYCHIATRIST TO ME AGAIN.

BUT EVIDENTLY, HE CONTINUED TO GO.

vs.
BRUCE ALLEN BECHDEL)   NO. 580-1

ORDER

AND NOW, this 2 day of april, 1975, it appearing to the court that the defendant, Bruce Allen Bechdel, has completed the terms of his Accelerated Rehabilitative Disposition Order, and that the District Attorney has no objections, the Defendant's application for dismissal of pending charges is hereby approved and it is ordered that all criminal charges be dismissed.
BY THE COURT:

MY MOTHER SAYS HE BEGAN COMING HOME FROM THE SESSIONS IN A FAMILIARLY MANIC MOOD.

I THOUGHT I'D ASK HIM UP FOR DINNER SOMETIME.

YOUR COUNSELOR? ARE YOU SERIOUS?

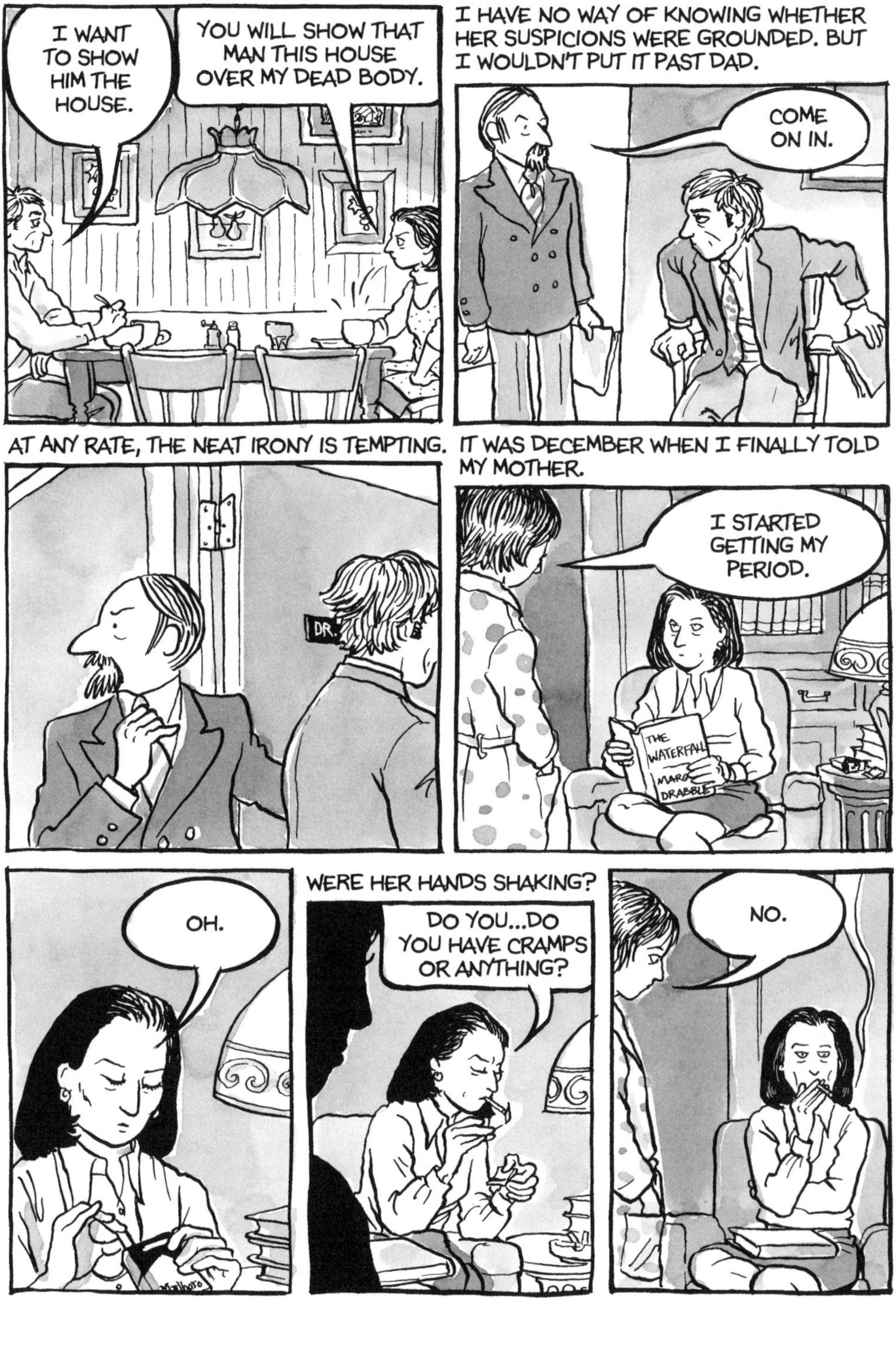
I WANT TO SHOW HIM THE HOUSE.
YOU WILL SHOW THAT MAN THIS HOUSE OVER MY DEAD BODY.
I HAVE NO WAY OF KNOWING WHETHER HER SUSPICIONS WERE GROUNDED. BUT I WOULDN'T PUT IT PAST DAD.
COME ON IN.
AT ANY RATE, THE NEAT IRONY IS TEMPTING.
DR.
IT WAS DECEMBER WHEN I FINALLY TOLD MY MOTHER.
I STARTED GETTING MY PERIOD.
THE WATERFALL
DRABBLE
OH.
WERE HER HANDS SHAKING?
DO YOU...DO YOU HAVE CRAMPS OR ANYTHING?
NO.

I'M ONLY ESTIMATING THAT THIS EPISODE TOOK PLACE IN DECEMBER. THERE'S NO MENTION OF IT IN MY DIARY.

BY THE END OF NOVEMBER, MY EARNEST DAILY ENTRIES HAD GIVEN WAY TO THE IMPLICIT LIE OF THE BLANK PAGE, AND WEEKS AT A TIME ARE LEFT UNRECORDED.

CHAPTER 7

THE ANTIHERO'S JOURNEY

IN 1976, DAD TOOK MY BROTHERS AND ME TO NEW YORK CITY FOR THE BICENTENNIAL.

AND ALSO TO SEE THE TALL SHIPS THAT HAD GATHERED FROM AROUND THE WORLD FOR THE OCCASION. MOM REMAINED AT HOME FOR A RUN OF *YOU CAN'T TAKE IT WITH YOU.*

WE STAYED AT HER FRIEND ELLY'S APARTMENT ON BLEECKER STREET, AS WE HAD ON NUMEROUS OTHER OCCASIONS.

BUT THIS TIME, AT AGE FIFTEEN, I SAW THE NEIGHBORHOOD IN A NEW LIGHT.

IT WAS LIKE THE MOMENT THE MANICURIST IN THE PALMOLIVE COMMERCIAL INFORMS HER CLIENT, "YOU'RE SOAKING IN IT."

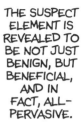

THE SUSPECT ELEMENT IS REVEALED TO BE NOT JUST BENIGN, BUT BENEFICIAL, AND IN FACT, ALL-PERVASIVE.

I WAS AS MOVED BY MY OWN OPEN-MINDED TOLERANCE AS I WAS BY THE ARRESTING DISPLAY OF COSMETICIZED MASCULINITY.

IT WAS QUITE A GAY WEEKEND ALL AROUND. WE WENT TO THE BALLET.

BARYSHNIKOV

ELLY TOOK DAD AND ME TO SEE HER FRIENDS RICHARD AND TOM. ALTHOUGH NO ONE ACTUALLY SAID SO, I ASSUMED THAT THEY WERE A COUPLE.

RICHARD WAS ILLUSTRATING A CHILDREN'S FILMSTRIP ABOUT PINOCCHIO.

I WAS GETTING REALLY BORED, BUT THEN I REALIZED I DIDN'T HAVE TO DRAW THE PICTURES IN ORDER.

MARKER ENVY

WE SOMEHOW GOT TICKETS TO *A CHORUS LINE*, WHICH HAD JUST SWEPT THE TONYS.

ONE DAY I LOOKED AT MYSELF IN THE MIRROR AND SAID, "YOU'RE FOURTEEN YEARS OLD AND YOU'RE A FAGGOT. WHAT ARE YOU GOING TO DO WITH YOUR LIFE?"

I DID NOT DRAW A CONSCIOUS PARALLEL TO MY OWN SEXUALITY, MUCH LESS TO MY FATHER'S.

...IT WAS PROBABLY THE FIRST TIME I REALIZED I WAS HOMOSEXUAL AND I GOT SO DEPRESSED BECAUSE I THOUGHT BEING GAY MEANT BEING A BUM ALL THE REST OF MY LIFE AND I SAID...

BUT THE IMMERSION--LIKE GREEN DISHWASHING LIQUID BATHING A CUTICLE--LEFT ME SUPPLE AND OPEN TO POSSIBILITY.

♪ I'LL NEVER GET TO WEAR NICE CLOTHES! ♪

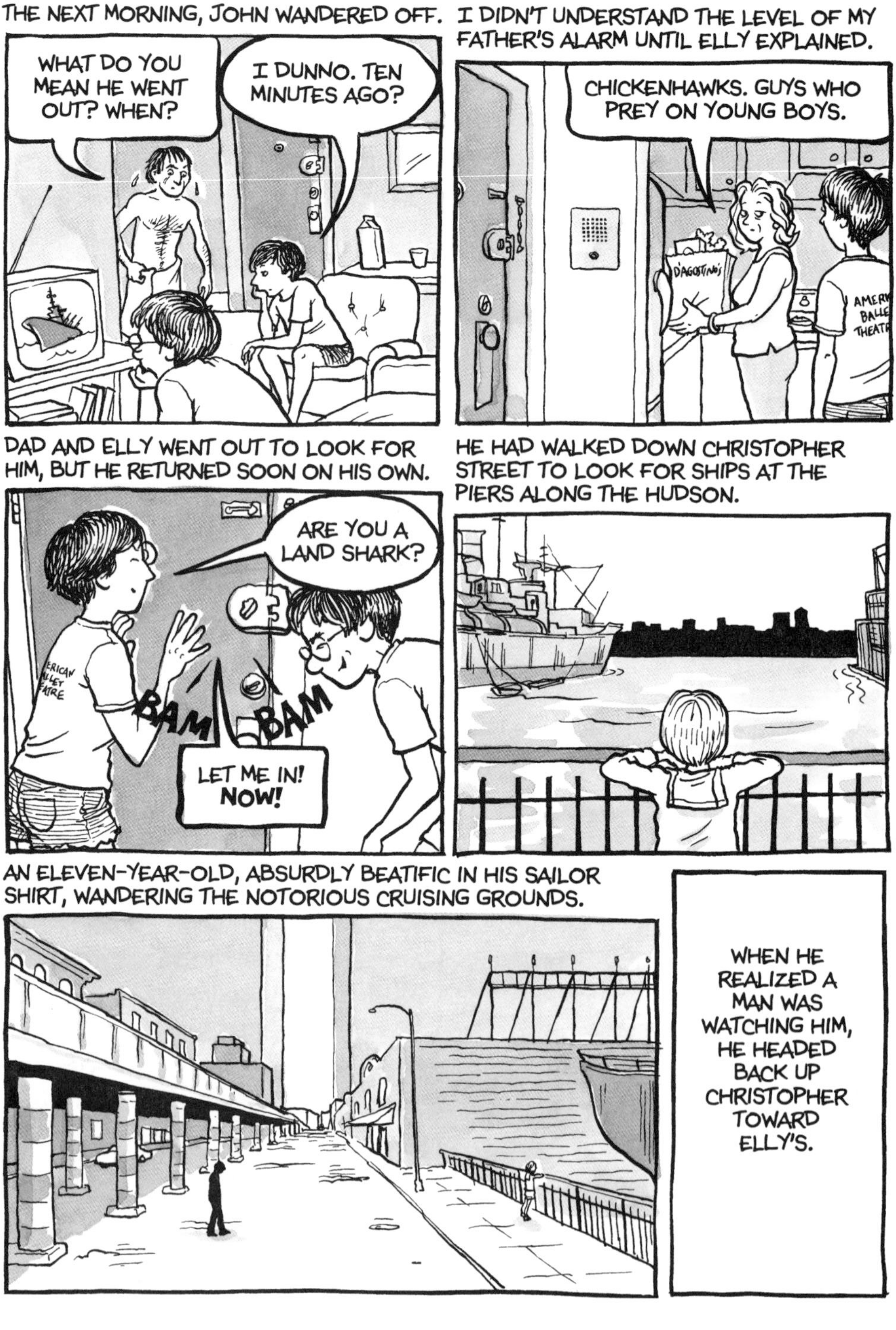
THE NEXT MORNING, JOHN WANDERED OFF.
WHAT DO YOU MEAN HE WENT OUT? WHEN?
I DUNNO. TEN MINUTES AGO?
I DIDN'T UNDERSTAND THE LEVEL OF MY FATHER'S ALARM UNTIL ELLY EXPLAINED.
CHICKENHAWKS. GUYS WHO PREY ON YOUNG BOYS.
D'AGOSTINO'S
AMERI BALLE THEATR
DAD AND ELLY WENT OUT TO LOOK FOR HIM, BUT HE RETURNED SOON ON HIS OWN.
ARE YOU A LAND SHARK?
BAM BAM
LET ME IN! NOW!
ERICAN LLET EATRE
HE HAD WALKED DOWN CHRISTOPHER STREET TO LOOK FOR SHIPS AT THE PIERS ALONG THE HUDSON.
AN ELEVEN-YEAR-OLD, ABSURDLY BEATIFIC IN HIS SAILOR SHIRT, WANDERING THE NOTORIOUS CRUISING GROUNDS.
WHEN HE REALIZED A MAN WAS WATCHING HIM, HE HEADED BACK UP CHRISTOPHER TOWARD ELLY'S.

THE MAN FOLLOWED.

YOU LIKE BOATS?

YEAH.

INSTINCTIVELY, JOHN HUMORED HIM UNTIL THEY NEARED THE APARTMENT.

I HAVE A BOAT.

UHH...WHAT KIND?

WE COULD GO SEE IT. IF IT'S OKAY WITH YOUR PARENTS.

MAYBE. I DUNNO...

WHEN THEY REACHED THE INTERSECTION WITH BLEECKER, JOHN BOLTED FROM HIM AS FAST AS HE COULD GO.

I DIDN'T KNOW ABOUT THE MAN UNTIL YEARS LATER. OR MAYBE I DID KNOW AND BLOCKED IT OUT, OR SIMPLY FORGOT BECAUSE THERE WAS SO MUCH ELSE GOING ON.

YOU **CANNOT** GO OUT BY YOURSELF.

I WANT EVERYONE READY TO LEAVE IN FIVE MINUTES FOR THE FRICK COLLECTION.

AT ANY RATE, WHEN DAD GOT BACK TO THE APARTMENT, HE WAS UNCHARACTERISTICALLY EAGER TO FORGIVE AND FORGET.

ELLY LEFT ON HER OWN VACATION AND WE STAYED FOR A FEW MORE DAYS. ON THE FOURTH, WE WATCHED THE TALL SHIPS AS THEY SAILED UP THE HUDSON.

WE HAD A DISAPPOINTING VIEW OF THE SPECTACLE, BUT AN EXCELLENT ONE OF THE CROWD AT THE PIERS.

WE HAD A SIMILARLY OBSTRUCTED VIEW OF THE FIREWORKS FROM THE ROOF THAT NIGHT.

THEN WE GOT READY FOR BED.

WHERE ARE YOU GOING?

OUT FOR A DRINK. I'LL BE BACK IN A LITTLE BIT. GO TO SLEEP.

AND IN SPITE OF THE CITY'S LITERALLY EXPLOSIVE ENERGY THAT NIGHT, I DID.

WHEN I TRY TO PROJECT WHAT DAD'S LIFE MIGHT HAVE BEEN LIKE IF HE HADN'T DIED IN 1980, I DON'T GET VERY FAR.

IF HE'D LIVED INTO THOSE EARLY YEARS OF AIDS, I TELL MYSELF, I MIGHT VERY WELL HAVE LOST HIM ANY-WAY, AND IN A MORE PAINFUL, PROTRACTED FASHION.

INDEED, IN THAT SCENARIO, I MIGHT HAVE LOST MY MOTHER TOO. PERHAPS I'M BEING HISTRIONIC, TRYING TO DISPLACE MY ACTUAL GRIEF WITH THIS IMAGINARY TRAUMA.

ALISON, YOU CAN TAKE OFF. WE'LL PUT IT TO BED TOMORROW.

BUT IS IT SO FAR-FETCHED? AND *THE BAND PLAYED ON*, THAT MINUTE CHRONICLE OF THE EARLY YEARS OF THE EPIDEMIC, OPENS ORGIASTICALLY AT THE BICENTENNIAL.

July 4, 1976
NEW YORK HARBOR

Tall sails scraped the deep purple night as rockers burst, flared, and flourished red, white, and blue over the stoic Statue of Liberty. The whole world was watching, it seemed; the whole world was there. Ships from fifty-five nations had poured sailors into Manhattan to join the throngs, counted in the millions, who watched the greatest pyrotechnic extravaganza ever mounted, all for America's 200th birthday party. Deep into the morning, bars all over the city were crammed with sailors. New York City had hosted the greatest party ever known, everybody agreed later. The guests had come from all over the world.

This was the part the epidemiologists would later note, when they stayed up late at night and the conversation drifted toward where it had started and when. They would remember that glorious night in New York Harbor, all those sailors, and recall: From all over the world they came to New York.

OR MAYBE I'M TRYING TO RENDER MY SENSELESS PERSONAL LOSS MEANINGFUL BY LINKING IT, HOWEVER POSTHUMOUSLY, TO A MORE COHERENT NARRATIVE.

A NARRATIVE OF INJUSTICE, OF SEXUAL SHAME AND FEAR, OF LIFE CONSIDERED EXPENDABLE.

IT'S TEMPTING TO SAY THAT, IN FACT, THIS **IS** MY FATHER'S STORY.

THERE'S A CERTAIN EMOTIONAL EXPEDIENCE TO CLAIMING HIM AS A TRAGIC VICTIM OF HOMOPHOBIA. BUT THAT'S A PROBLEMATIC LINE OF THOUGHT.

FOR ONE THING, IT MAKES IT HARDER FOR ME TO BLAME HIM.

196

AND FOR ANOTHER, IT LEADS TO A PECULIARLY LITERAL CUL DE SAC. IF MY FATHER HAD "COME OUT" IN HIS YOUTH, IF HE HAD NOT MET AND MARRIED MY MOTHER...

...WHERE WOULD THAT LEAVE ME?

WHAT IS A FATHER? EVEN THE DICTIONARY CONVEYS VAGUENESS AND DISTANCE.

OMINOUS — fate·ful·ly \'fā-le\ adv — fate·ful·ness n
¹fa·ther \'fǟth-ər\ n [ME fader, fr OE fæder; akin to OHG fater father, L pater, Gk patēr] 1 a : a man who has begotten a child : SIRE b cap (1) : ²GOD (2) : the first person of the Trinity

LOOKING UP THE ARCHAIC PARTICIPLE DOESN'T YIELD MUCH MORE THAN A TAUTOLOGY.

be·gat \bi-'gat\ archaic past of BEGET
be·get \bi-'get\ vt be·got \-'gät\ be·got·ten \-'gät-ᵊn\ or begot; be·get·ting [ME begeten, alter. of beyeten, fr. OE bigietan] 1 : to procreate as the father : SIRE 2 : CAUSE — be·get·ter n
beg·gar \'beg-ər\ n [ME beggere, beggare, fr. beggen to beg +

IN MY EARLIEST MEMORIES, DAD IS A LOWERING, MALEVOLENT PRESENCE.

HIS ARRIVAL HOME FROM WORK CAST A COLD PALL ON THE PEACEABLE KINGDOM WHERE MOM, CHRISTIAN, AND I SPENT OUR DAYS.

TIME TO PUT THIS AWAY.

DAD DIDN'T HAVE MUCH USE FOR SMALL CHILDREN, BUT AS I GOT OLDER, HE BEGAN TO SENSE MY POTENTIAL AS AN INTELLECTUAL COMPANION.

WHEN ARE YOU GOING TO READ *CATCHER IN THE RYE*?

YEARS OF NEGLECT HAD LEFT ME WARY.

AFTER I PUT YOU IN THE NURSING HOME.

BUT THEN I ENDED UP IN HIS ENGLISH CLASS, A COURSE CALLED "RITES OF PASSAGE," AND I FOUND THAT I LIKED THE BOOKS DAD WANTED ME TO READ.

WHO'S MR. ANTOLINI? PETERS?

I DUNNO.

HE'S HOLDEN'S OLD ENGLISH TEACHER.

HOW DOES HOLDEN FEEL ABOUT HIM?

HE LIKES HIM. THAT'S WHY HE ASKS IF HE CAN STAY THERE.

AND DOES HE TURN OUT TO BE SUCH A GREAT GUY? WHAT HAPPENS?

ANYONE?

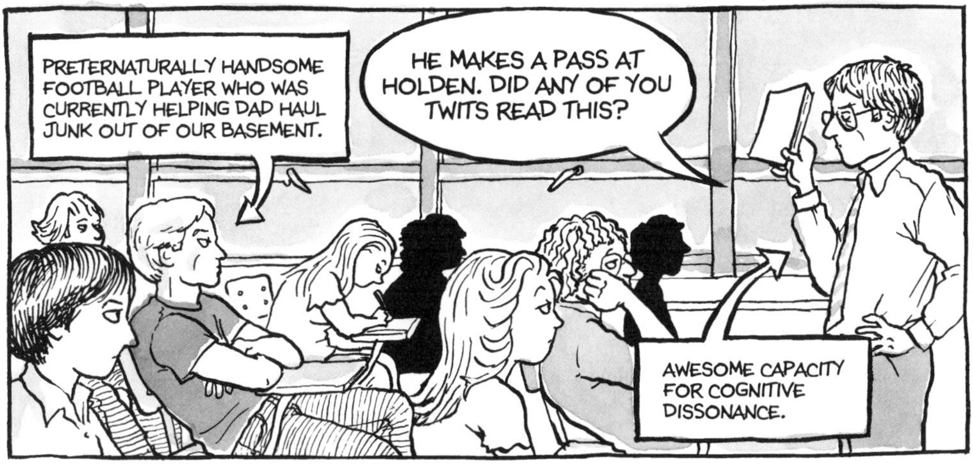
PRETERNATURALLY HANDSOME FOOTBALL PLAYER WHO WAS CURRENTLY HELPING DAD HAUL JUNK OUT OF OUR BASEMENT.
HE MAKES A PASS AT HOLDEN. DID ANY OF YOU TWITS READ THIS?
AWESOME CAPACITY FOR COGNITIVE DISSONANCE.

SOMETIMES IT WAS AS IF DAD AND I WERE THE ONLY ONES IN THE ROOM.

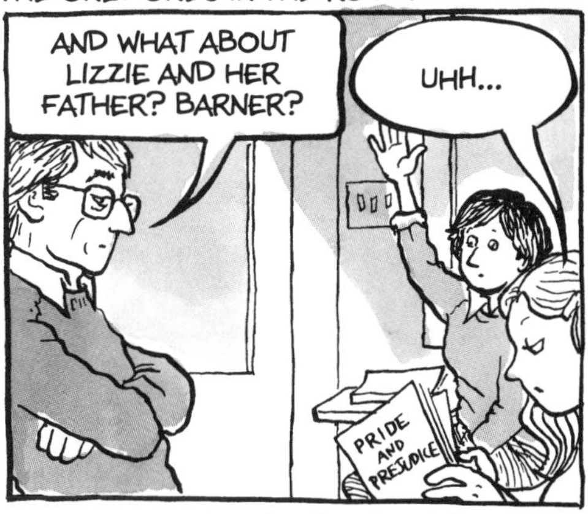
AND WHAT ABOUT LIZZIE AND HER FATHER? BARNER?
UHH...
PRIDE AND PREJUDICE

THE SENSATION OF INTIMACY WAS NOVEL.

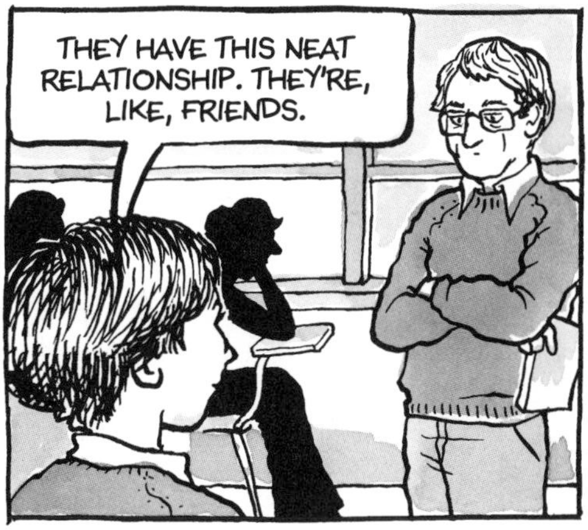
THEY HAVE THIS NEAT RELATIONSHIP. THEY'RE, LIKE, FRIENDS.

I THINK WE WERE BOTH STARVED FOR ATTENTION.

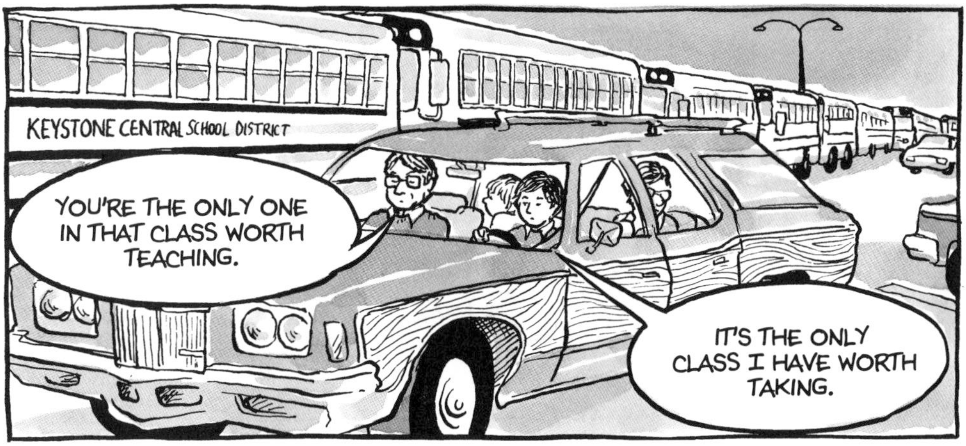
KEYSTONE CENTRAL SCHOOL DISTRICT
YOU'RE THE ONLY ONE IN THAT CLASS WORTH TEACHING.
IT'S THE ONLY CLASS I HAVE WORTH TAKING.

WE GREW EVEN CLOSER AFTER I WENT AWAY TO COLLEGE. BOOKS--THE ONES ASSIGNED FOR MY ENGLISH CLASS--CONTINUED TO SERVE AS OUR CURRENCY.

It's ironic that I am paying to send you North to study texts I'm teaching to high school twits. As I Lay Dying is one of the century's greatest. Faulkner IS Beech Creek. The Bundrens ARE Bechdels - 19th century perhaps but definitely kin. How about that dude's way with words. He knows how us country boys think and talk. If you ever -gawdforbid- get homesick, read Darl's monologue. In a strange room you must empty yourself for sleep...How often have I lain beneath rain on a strange roof... Darl had been to Paris you know - WWI.

AT FIRST I WAS GLAD FOR THE HELP. MY FRESHMAN ENGLISH CLASS, "MYTHOLOGY AND ARCHETYPAL EXPERIENCE," CONFOUNDED ME.

DO YOU SEE HOW JAKE'S RENEWAL IN SPAIN EXACTLY FOLLOWS THE PROCESS OF REBIRTH THAT JUNG CALLS "NATURAL TRANSFORMATION"?

I DIDN'T UNDERSTAND WHY WE COULDN'T JUST READ THE BOOKS WITHOUT FORCING CONTORTED INTERPRETATIONS ON THEM.

I WAS NOT ALONE IN FAILING TO GRASP THE SYMBOLIC FUNCTION OF LITERATURE.

YOU MEAN, LIKE... HEMINGWAY DID THAT ON PURPOSE?

OUR TEACHER FREQUENTLY GREW EXASPERATED WITH THE WHOLE CLASS.

GET IT? MARLOW'S STEAMER? PENIS. THE CONGO? VAGINA.

200

OUR PAPERS CAME BACK BLOODIED WITH RED MARKS--MOST LAVISHLY THE WITHERING "WW" FOR "WRONG WORD."

"IS"? HOW CAN "IS" BE WRONG?

BUT LIKE A BATTERED BOXER, I KEPT SWINGING, BUOYED UP BY MY FATHER'S ENERGETIC COACHING FROM THE CORNER.

OKAY, LET'S TALK ABOUT *THE SUN ALSO RISES*. IT'S A ROMAN À CLEF, RIGHT? JAKE IS HEMINGWAY. COHN WAS A GUY NAMED HAROLD LOEB. BRETT IS A LADY DUFF TWYSDEN.

THOUGH NOW THAT I THINK OF IT, IT'S UNCLEAR WHETHER HE WAS THE VICARIOUS TEACHER OR THE VICARIOUS STUDENT.

THEY SAY SHE STARTED THE NEW LOOK FOR WOMEN, WITH SHORT HAIR AND MEN'S CLOTHES. AND SHE REALLY DID HAVE AN AFFAIR WITH LOEB BEFORE MEETING UP WITH HIM AND HEMINGWAY IN PAMPLONA. YOU KNOW, ANDY, THE BEST MAN AT OUR WEDDING, SAW HEMINGWAY IN PAMPLONA THE YEAR BEFORE WE WERE MARRIED.

EVENTUALLY, HIS EXCITEMENT BEGAN TO LEAVE LITTLE ROOM FOR MY OWN.

HE'D JUST COME FROM PARIS WHERE HE WAS HANGING OUT WITH SYLVIA BEACH AND JAMES JOYCE. BEACH RAN THE FAMOUS BOOKSTORE SHAKE-SPEARE AND COMPANY, AND PUBLISHED *ULYSSES*. I MET HER ONCE IN PARIS.

AND BY THE END OF THE YEAR I WAS SUFFOCATING.

WHAT ARE YOU READING NEXT?

A PORTRAIT OF THE ARTIST AS A YOUNG MAN.

GOOD. YOU DAMN WELL BETTER IDENTIFY WITH EVERY PAGE.

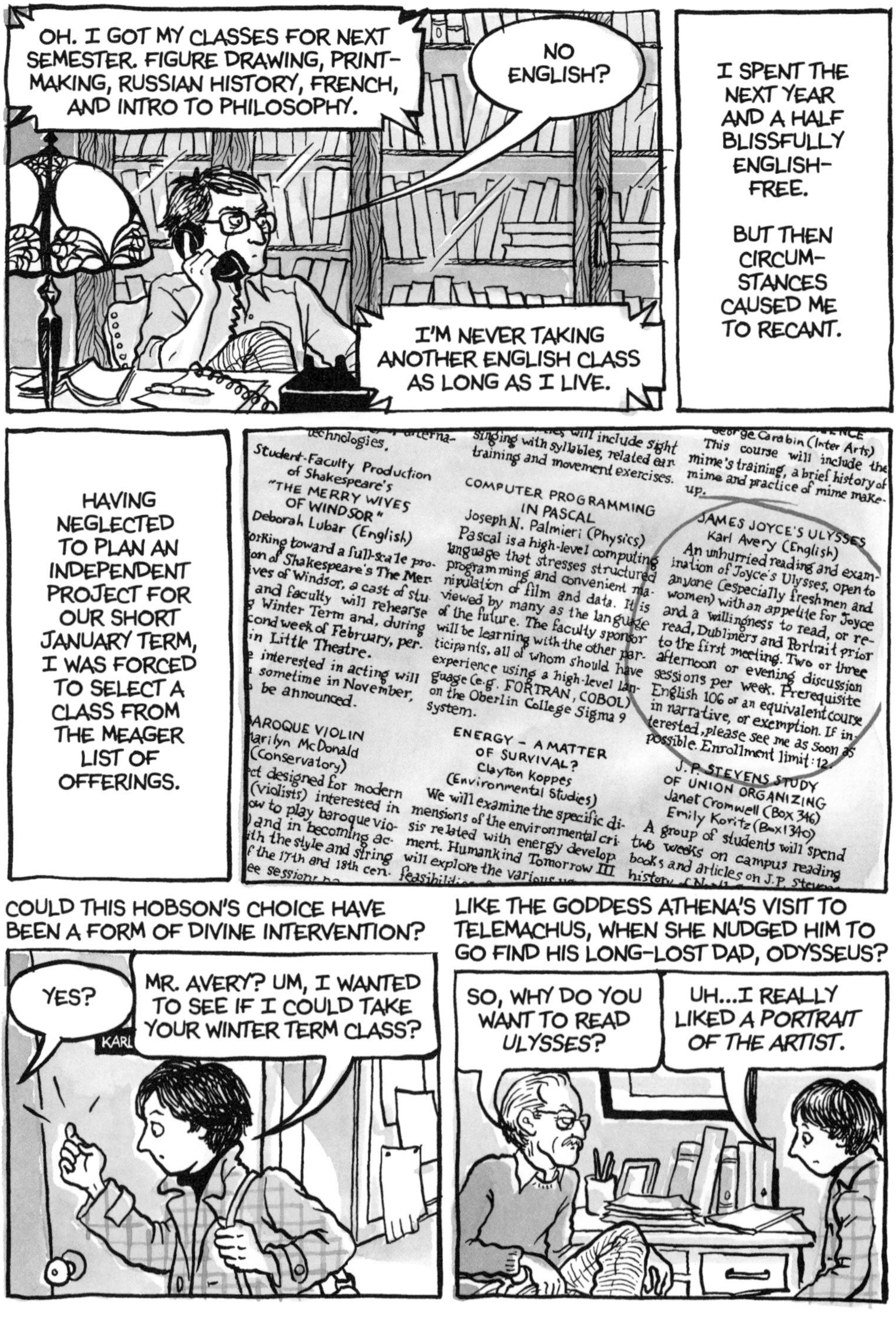
OH. I GOT MY CLASSES FOR NEXT SEMESTER. FIGURE DRAWING, PRINTMAKING, RUSSIAN HISTORY, FRENCH, AND INTRO TO PHILOSOPHY.
NO ENGLISH?
I'M NEVER TAKING ANOTHER ENGLISH CLASS AS LONG AS I LIVE.
I SPENT THE NEXT YEAR AND A HALF BLISSFULLY ENGLISH-FREE.
BUT THEN CIRCUMSTANCES CAUSED ME TO RECANT.
HAVING NEGLECTED TO PLAN AN INDEPENDENT PROJECT FOR OUR SHORT JANUARY TERM, I WAS FORCED TO SELECT A CLASS FROM THE MEAGER LIST OF OFFERINGS.
technologies.
Student-Faculty Production of Shakespeare's "THE MERRY WIVES OF WINDSOR"
Deborah Lubar (English)
orking toward a full-scale pro- on of Shakespeare's The Mer- ives of Windsor, a cast of stu- and faculty will rehearse g Winter Term and, during cond week of February, per- in Little Theatre. e interested in acting will sometime in November, be announced.
AROQUE VIOLIN
arilyn McDonald (Conservatory)
ct designed for modern (violists) interested in ow to play baroque vio- and in becoming ac- ith the style and string f the 17th and 18th cen-
singing with syllables, related ear training and movement exercises.
COMPUTER PROGRAMMING IN PASCAL
Joseph N. Palmieri (Physics)
Pascal is a high-level computing language that stresses structured programming and convenient manipulation of film and data. It is viewed by many as the language of the future. The faculty sponsor will be learning with the other participants, all of whom should have experience using a high-level language (e.g. FORTRAN, COBOL) on the Oberlin College Sigma 9 system.
ENERGY – A MATTER OF SURVIVAL?
Clayton Koppes (Environmental Studies)
We will examine the specific dimensions of the environmental crisis related with energy development. Humankind Tomorrow III will explore the various
George Carabin (Inter Arts)
This course will include the mime's training, a brief history of mime and practice of mime make-up.
JAMES JOYCE'S ULYSSES
Karl Avery (English)
An unhurried reading and examination of Joyce's Ulysses, open to anyone (especially freshmen and women) with an appetite for Joyce and a willingness to read, or re-read, Dubliners and Portrait prior to the first meeting. Two or three afternoon or evening discussion sessions per week. Prerequisite English 106 or an equivalent course in narrative, or exemption. If interested, please see me as soon as possible. Enrollment limit: 12.
J. P. STEVENS STUDY OF UNION ORGANIZING
Janet Cromwell (Box 346)
Emily Koritz (Box 1340)
A group of students will spend two weeks on campus reading books and articles on J.P. Stevens
COULD THIS HOBSON'S CHOICE HAVE BEEN A FORM OF DIVINE INTERVENTION?
YES?
MR. AVERY? UM, I WANTED TO SEE IF I COULD TAKE YOUR WINTER TERM CLASS?
KARL
LIKE THE GODDESS ATHENA'S VISIT TO TELEMACHUS, WHEN SHE NUDGED HIM TO GO FIND HIS LONG-LOST DAD, ODYSSEUS?
SO, WHY DO YOU WANT TO READ *ULYSSES*?
UH...I REALLY LIKED *A PORTRAIT OF THE ARTIST*.

FOR I WAS BEGGING ADMISSION TO NOT JUST ANY ENGLISH CLASS, BUT ONE DEVOTED TO MY FATHER'S FAVORITE BOOK OF ALL TIME.

SO YOU HAVEN'T TAKEN ANY LITERATURE COURSES SINCE YOUR FRESHMAN YEAR?

THE DESCENT OF MINERVA

JOHN FLAXMAN

NO. BUT, UM... I STILL READ.

THAT'S FINE. JUST MAKE SURE TO REVIEW *PORTRAIT* AND *DUBLINERS* BEFORE CLASS STARTS.

REMARKABLY, THIS INTERVIEW WITH MR. AVERY OCCURRED ON THE SELFSAME AFTERNOON THAT I REALIZED, IN THE CAMPUS BOOKSTORE, THAT I WAS A LESBIAN.

AND INDEED, I EMBARKED THAT DAY ON AN ODYSSEY WHICH, CONSISTING AS IT DID IN A GRADUAL, EPISODIC, AND INEVITABLE CONVERGENCE WITH MY ABSTRACTED FATHER, WAS VERY NEARLY AS EPIC AS THE ORIGINAL.

HOME FOR CHRISTMAS, I FOUND DAD'S DELIGHT ABOUT *ULYSSES* A BIT GALLING.

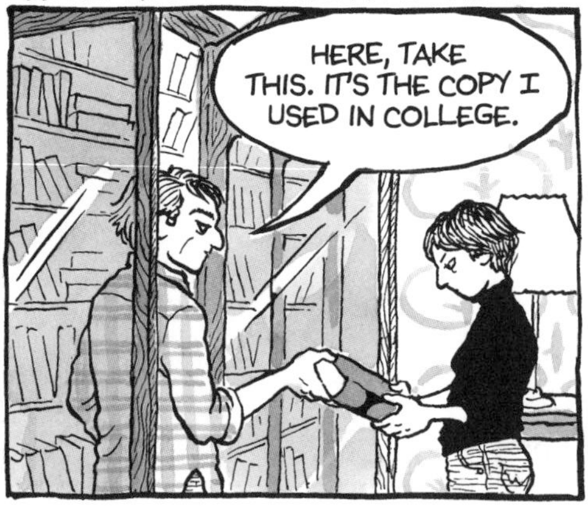
HERE, TAKE THIS. IT'S THE COPY I USED IN COLLEGE.

BUT IT WAS NICE TO HAVE HIS ATTENTION.

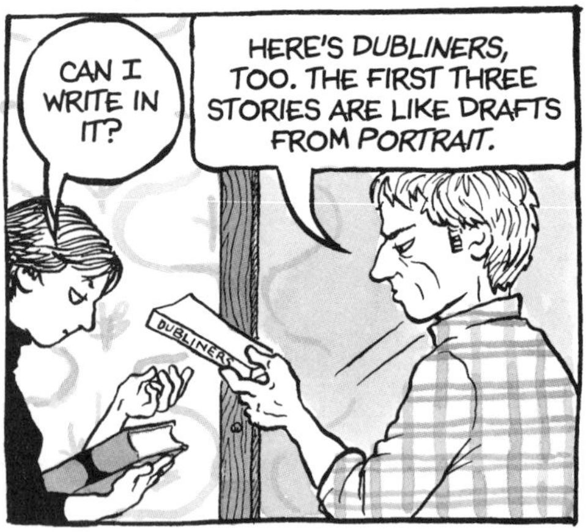
CAN I WRITE IN IT?
HERE'S *DUBLINERS*, TOO. THE FIRST THREE STORIES ARE LIKE DRAFTS FROM *PORTRAIT*.
DUBLINERS

I REALIZED I HAD MISSED IT, HOWEVER VICARIOUS IT MAY HAVE BEEN.

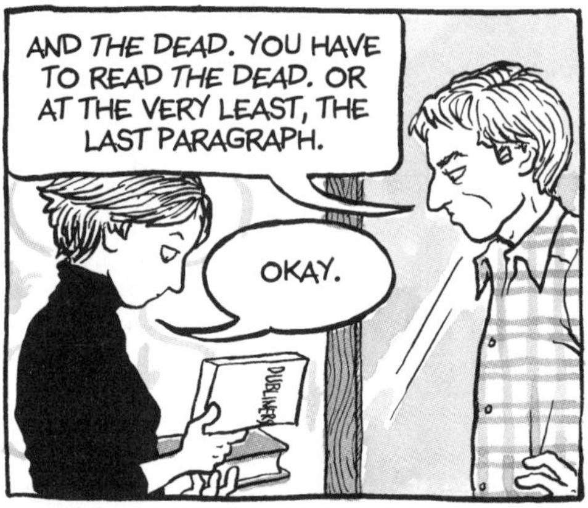
AND *THE DEAD*. YOU HAVE TO READ *THE DEAD*. OR AT THE VERY LEAST, THE LAST PARAGRAPH.
OKAY.
DUBLINERS

IN A BURST OF TENDERNESS, I ENCOURAGED HIM FURTHER.

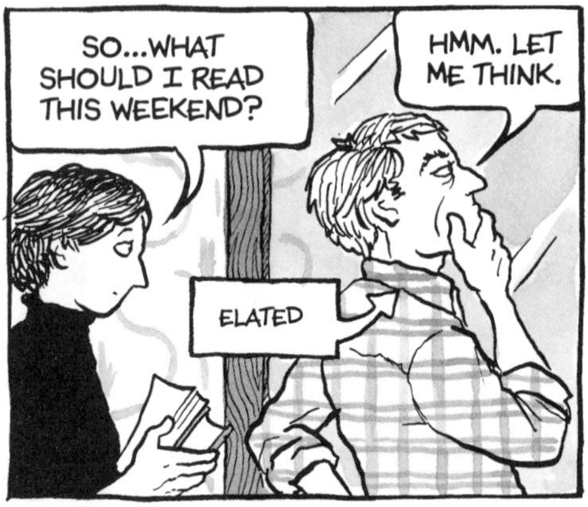
SO...WHAT SHOULD I READ THIS WEEKEND?
HMM. LET ME THINK.
ELATED

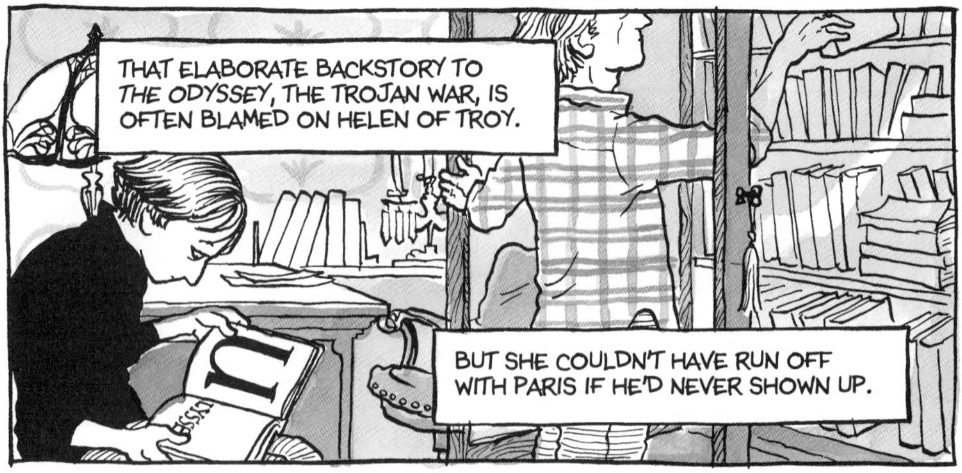
THAT ELABORATE BACKSTORY TO *THE ODYSSEY*, THE TROJAN WAR, IS OFTEN BLAMED ON HELEN OF TROY.
BUT SHE COULDN'T HAVE RUN OFF WITH PARIS IF HE'D NEVER SHOWN UP.

PARIS PLAYS A SIMILARLY INCITING ROLE IN MY ODYSSEY TOO.

YOU SHOULD LEARN ABOUT PARIS IN THE TWENTIES, THAT WHOLE SCENE.

COLETTE'S AUTO-BIOGRAPHY

EARTHLY PARADISE

EARTHLY PARADISE Colette

CLOVE CIGARETTE

I HADN'T MENTIONED MY BIG LESBIAN EPIPHANY YET. SO DAD'S CHOICE WAS INTERESTING, TO SAY THE LEAST.

...noted, her name was repeated in the midst of a subdued and almost subterranean tumult, was heard especially in the friendly little dives, the tiny, neighborhood cinemas frequented by groups of her women friends—basement rooms arranged as restaurants, dim, and blue with tobacco smoke. There was also a cellar in Montmartre that welcomed these uneasy women haunted by their own solitude, who felt safe within the low-ceilinged room beneath the eye of a frank proprietress who shared their predilections, while an unctuous and authentic cheese fondue sputtered and the loud contralto of an artiste, one of...

WE DID NOT DISCUSS THE BOOK. IN JANUARY I BROUGHT IT BACK TO SCHOOL AND ADDED IT TO MY GROWING STACK.

LESBIAN/WOMAN
Orlando·WOOLF
RUBYFRUIT JUNGLE
The WELL of LONELINESS
DESERT OF THE HEART ·· RULE
CECIL BEATON'S DIARIES
THE HOMOSEXUAL MATRIX · C.A.TRIPP

IF ONLY I'D HAD THE FORESIGHT TO CALL THIS AN INDEPENDENT READING.

"CONTEMPORARY AND HISTORICAL PERSPECTIVES ON HOMO-SEXUALITY" WOULD HAVE HAD QUITE A LEGITIMATE RING.

BUT ALAS, 768 PAGES OF *ULYSSES* LAY BEFORE ME LIKE AN EXPANSE OF UNCHARTED SEA. THE CLASS MET IN PROFESSOR AVERY'S LIVING ROOM.

SO, JUST LIKE IN *THE ODYSSEY*, THE FIRST THREE CHAPTERS FOCUS ON THE SON'S EXPERIENCE--OUR OLD FRIEND STEPHEN DEDALUS.

MR. AVERY HAD HURT HIS BACK, AND RECLINED ON THE COUCH MUCH AS THE WISE WINDBAG, NESTOR, MIGHT HAVE RECLINED WHILE COUNSELING YOUNG TELEMACHUS.

I STILL FOUND LITERARY CRITICISM TO BE A SUSPECT ACTIVITY.

NOW IF ONE OF JOYCE'S THEMES IS PATERNITY, THEN WHY IS THE STORY ABOUT STEPHEN AND BLOOM, WHO ARE VIRTUAL STRANGERS, AND NOT ABOUT STEPHEN'S ACTUAL, PHYSICAL FATHER?

BECAUSE THAT'D BE TOO SIMPLE.

BLOOM IS STEPHEN'S SPIRITUAL FATHER.

...AND LIKE ULYSSES, BOTH STEPHEN AND BLOOM ARE EXILES. STEPHEN BECAUSE HE'S AN ARTIST. BLOOM BECAUSE HE'S A JEW.

ALSO, IT TOOK ULYSSES TEN YEARS TO GET HOME, AND IT'S BEEN TEN YEARS SINCE BLOOM HAD SEX WITH HIS WIFE.

ONCE YOU GRASPED THAT *ULYSSES* WAS BASED ON *THE ODYSSEY*, WAS IT REALLY NECESSARY TO ENUMERATE EVERY LAST POINT OF CORRESPONDENCE?

MAYBE SO. WITHOUT THE HOMERIC CLUES, IT WOULD CERTAINLY BE UNREADABLE.

BUT THEN, I HAD LITTLE PATIENCE FOR JOYCE'S DIVAGATIONS WHEN MY OWN ODYSSEY WAS CALLING SO SEDUCTIVELY.

IF I WAS BEWITCHED, IT WAS NOT AN UNPLEASANT SENSATION.

ONE SIREN LED TO ANOTHER IN AN INTERTEXTUAL PROGRESSION.

...IN THAT SPIRIT OF MARVELOUS MEGALO-MANIA I CAME OUT OFFICIALLY JULY 1ST (1970) IN THE *VOICE* IN A PIECE TITLED AMBIVALENTLY FROM A LINE BY COLETTE "OF THIS PURE BUT IRREGULAR PASSION."

I REFERRED BACK TO COLETTE HERSELF, BASKING IN HER SENSUALISM AS PER-HAPS THE SEA-RAVAGED ODYSSEUS HAD IN THE MINISTRATIONS OF NAUSICAA.

BUT COLETTE ALSO HAD HER DECIDEDLY ANAPHRODISIAC MOMENTS.

GENERAL CH

IN ONE BREATH SHE DESCRIBES A SEVENTEEN-YEAR-OLD BUTCHER BOY...

decked out in a dress of black Chantilly lace over pale blue silk, his face sulky beneath a wide lace hat, as uncouth as a country wench in need of a husband, his cheeks plump and fresh as nectarines

AND IN THE NEXT, WITH THE SAME VOLUPTUOUS DETAIL, SHE REPORTS HIS SUICIDE.

He shattered with a revolver bullet his pretty, pouting mouth, his low forehead beneath kinky hair, his anxious and timid little bright blue eyes.

I FELL FURTHER AND FURTHER BEHIND IN *ULYSSES*.

BUT I ATTENDED CLASS RELIGIOUSLY.

NOW, I'M SURE THE CATHOLICS IN THE CLASS WILL RECOGNIZE THE NARRATIVE TECHNIQUE OF THE ITHACA CHAPTER.

WE WILL?

"WHAT, REDUCED TO THEIR SIMPLEST RECIPROCAL FORM, WERE BLOOM'S THOUGHTS ABOUT STEPHEN'S THOUGHTS ABOUT BLOOM AND BLOOM'S THOUGHTS ABOUT STEPHEN'S THOUGHTS ABOUT BLOOM'S THOUGHTS ABOUT STEPHEN?"

"HE THOUGHT THAT HE THOUGHT THAT HE WAS A JEW WHEREAS HE KNEW THAT HE KNEW THAT HE KNEW THAT HE WAS NOT."

COME ON. "WHO MADE YOU? GOD MADE ME." RING A BELL?

CATECHISM!

EXACTLY. BUT EVEN WITH THE DETAILED SCIENTIFIC ANSWERS THAT THIS CATECHISM PROVIDES, DO WE LEARN ANYTHING CONCRETE ABOUT BLOOM AND STEPHEN'S ENCOUNTER? DO THEY CONNECT?

What did each do at the door of egress?
Bloom set the candlestick on the floor. Stephen put the hat on his head.

For what creature was the door of e-
For a cat.

What specia... confro...
[682]

I HAD NO IDEA. BY THE TIME THE JANUARY TERM ENDED, I STILL HAD TWO HUNDRED PAGES TO GO.

AND LIKE ODYSSEUS'S MEN WHO HAD FALLEN IN WITH THE LOTUS-EATERS, I FELT NO URGENCY TO CONTINUE.

The Letters of VIRGINIA WOOLF

m&m's

THE REGULAR SEMESTER BEGAN AND I STILL HADN'T MET WITH MR. AVERY FOR MY ORAL EXAM ON *ULYSSES*.

235
GAY UNION

I HAD A MORE DAUNTING TEST TO FACE FIRST: DESCENT INTO THE UNDERWORLD.

209

IT WAS A BENIGN AND WELL-LIT UNDERWORLD, ADMITTEDLY, BUT ODYSSEUS SAILING TO HADES COULD NOT HAVE FELT MORE TREPIDATION THAN I DID ENTERING THAT ROOM.

NOR COULD HE HAVE BEEN MORE TRANSFORMED BY THE INITIATION THAT BEFELL HIM THERE. IN THE WEEK AFTER THE MEETING, MY QUEST SHIFTED ABRUPTLY OUTWARD.

I'M A LESBIAN.

COOL! CAN I TELL MY FRIENDS?

ROOMMATE

n a lesbian

MY PARENTS RECEIVED THE LETTER ON THE SAME DAY THAT I BULLSHIT MY WAY THROUGH THE *ULYSSES* EXAM.

DAD CALLED THAT EVENING. IF HE HAD MENTIONED HIS OWN HOMOSEXUALITY AT THIS JUNCTURE, IT MIGHT HAVE EXPLAINED HIS ODDLY PROCURESS-LIKE TONE.

UM, BLOOM IS LIKE HIS SPIRITUAL FATHER, Y'KNOW?

AT LEAST YOU'RE HUMAN. EVERYONE SHOULD EXPERIMENT.

LIKE STEPHEN AND BLOOM AT THE NATIONAL LIBRARY, OUR PATHS CROSSED BUT WE DID NOT MEET.

DO YOU HAVE TO PUT A LABEL ON YOURSELF?

FILM SERIE
ERNST LUBITSCH

IT WASN'T UNTIL THREE WEEKS LATER THAT MOM LET ME IN ON THE BIG SECRET.

ROY, OUR **BABY-SITTER?**

UNMOORED AS I STILL WAS BY MY OWN QUEERNESS, THIS BROADSIDE SWAMPED MY SMALL CRAFT.

I WONDER IF GIRLS CAN JOIN THE MERCHANT MARINE?

HANDEL: WASSERMUSIK

disc

AND A LETTER FROM DAD THE NEXT DAY LEFT ME EVEN MORE AWASH.

INSTEAD OF AT LAST CONFIDING IN ME, HE TOOK THE NOVEL APPROACH OF ASSUMING THAT I ALREADY KNEW--ALTHOUGH AT THE TIME HE WROTE THE LETTER, I DID NOT.

Helen just seems to be suggesting that you keep your options open. I tend to go along with that but probably for different reasons. Of course, it seems like a cop out. But then, who are cop outs for? Taking sides is rahther heroic, and I am not a hero. What is really worth it?

There've been a few times I thought I might have preferred to take a stand. But I never really considered it when I was young. In fact, I don't htink I ever considered it till I was over thirty. let's face it things do look different then. At forty-three I find it hard to see advantages even if I had done so when I was young.

WHAT, REDUCED TO THEIR SIMPLEST RECIPROCAL FORM, WERE DAD'S THOUGHTS ABOUT MY THOUGHTS ABOUT HIM, AND HIS THOUGHTS ABOUT MY THOUGHTS ABOUT HIS THOUGHTS ABOUT ME?

HEY!

UH...HI.

LET'S START A PEOPLE-LIKE-US TABLE.

SOME OF MY NEW ASSOCIATES

HE THOUGHT THAT I THOUGHT THAT HE WAS A QUEER. WHEREAS HE KNEW THAT I KNEW THAT HE KNEW THAT I WAS TOO.

I'll admit that I have been somewhat envious of the "new" freedom (?) that appears on campuses today. In the fifties it was not even considered an option. It's hard to believe that just as it's hard to believe that I saw Colored and Whites on drinking fountains in Florida in elementary school. Yes, my world was quite limited. You know I was never even in New York until I was about twenty. But even seeing it then was not quite a revelation. There was not much in the Village that I hadn't known in Beech Creek. In New York you could see and mention it but elsewhere it was not seen or mentioned. It was rather simple.

I WAS ADRIFT ON THE HIGH SEAS, BUT MY COURSE WAS BECOMING CLEAR. IT LAY BE-
TWEEN THE SCYLLA OF MY PEERS AND THE SWIRLING, SUCKING CHARYBDIS OF MY FAMILY.

VEERING TOWARD SCYLLA SEEMED MUCH THE SAFER ROUTE. AND AFTER NAVIGATING THE PASSAGE, I SOON WASHED UP, A BIT STUNNED, ON A NEW SHORE.

(FROM A RECENT ONE-WOMAN PROTEST AGAINST SOME VISITING CHRISTIANS)

LESBIAN TERRORIST

KEEP YOUR GOD OFF MY BODY

LIKE ODYSSEUS ON THE ISLAND OF THE CYCLOPS, I FOUND MYSELF FACING A "BEING OF COLOSSAL STRENGTH AND FEROCITY, TO WHOM THE LAW OF MAN AND GOD MEANT NOTHING."

IN TRUE HEROIC FASHION, I MOVED TOWARD THE THING I FEARED.

YET WHILE ODYSSEUS SCHEMED DESPERATELY TO ESCAPE POLYPHEMUS'S CAVE, I FOUND THAT I WAS QUITE CONTENT TO STAY HERE FOREVER.

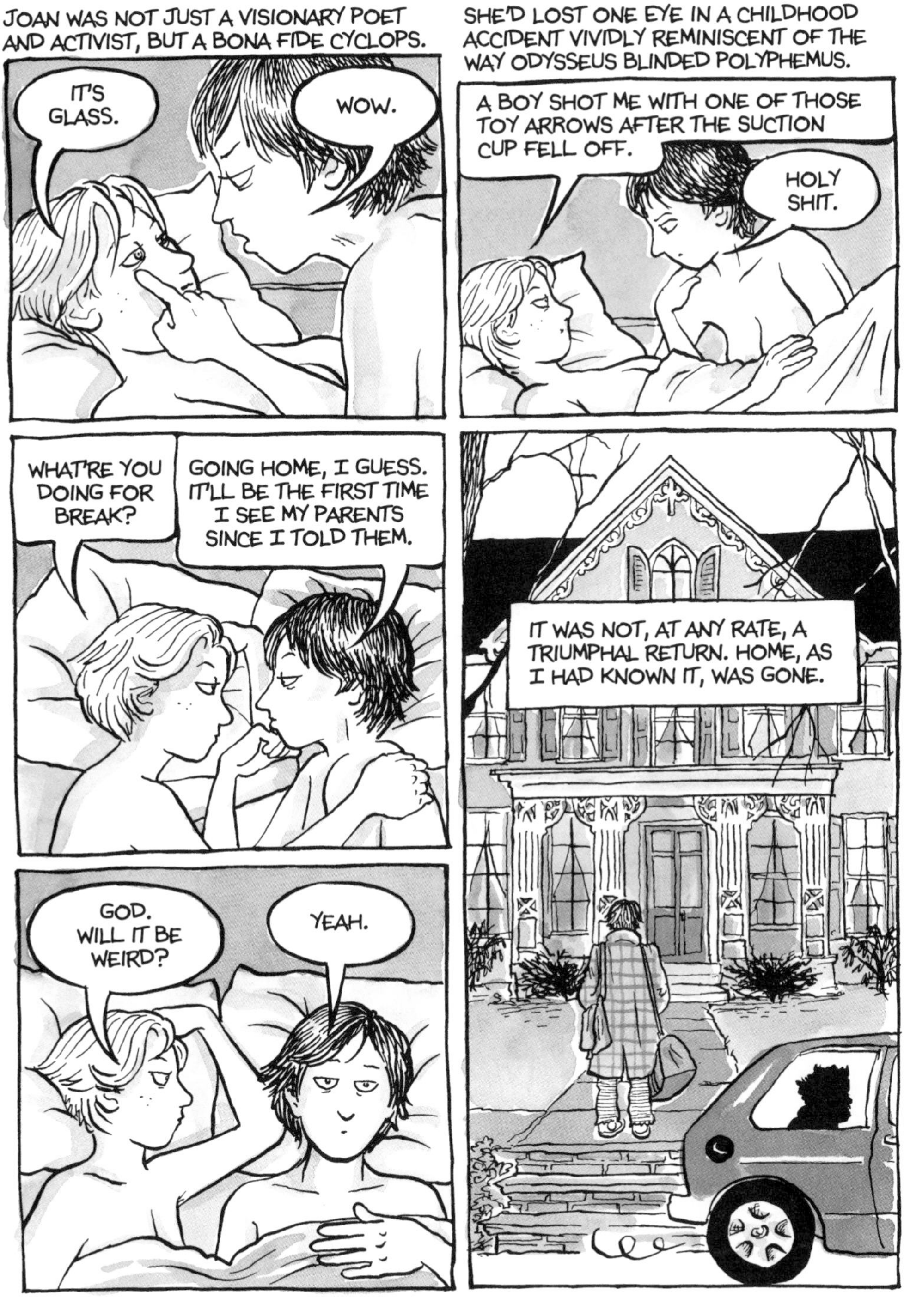
JOAN WAS NOT JUST A VISIONARY POET AND ACTIVIST, BUT A BONA FIDE CYCLOPS.
IT'S GLASS.
WOW.
SHE'D LOST ONE EYE IN A CHILDHOOD ACCIDENT VIVIDLY REMINISCENT OF THE WAY ODYSSEUS BLINDED POLYPHEMUS.
A BOY SHOT ME WITH ONE OF THOSE TOY ARROWS AFTER THE SUCTION CUP FELL OFF.
HOLY SHIT.
WHAT'RE YOU DOING FOR BREAK?
GOING HOME, I GUESS. IT'LL BE THE FIRST TIME I SEE MY PARENTS SINCE I TOLD THEM.
GOD. WILL IT BE WEIRD?
YEAH.
IT WAS NOT, AT ANY RATE, A TRIUMPHAL RETURN. HOME, AS I HAD KNOWN IT, WAS GONE.

SOME CRUCIAL PART OF THE STRUCTURE SEEMED TO BE MISSING, LIKE IN DREAMS I WOULD HAVE LATER WHERE TERMITES HAD EATEN THROUGH ALL THE FLOOR JOISTS.

I'M GOING OVER TO DOUG'S.

I'VE GOT A VIEWING.

SCOUT MEETING.

MOM TOOK ME INTO HER CONFIDENCE.

...AND WHEN WE'D GO TO NEW YORK, HE'D GO OUT ALONE AT NIGHT. ONCE HE GOT BODY LICE! BUT IT'S NOT JUST THE...THE...AFFAIRS. IT'S THE SHOPLIFTING, THE SPEEDING TICKETS, THE LYING, HIS RAGES.

LICE?

LIKE ODYSSEUS'S FAITHFUL PENELOPE, MY MOTHER HAD KEPT THE HOUSEHOLD GOING FOR TWENTY YEARS WITH A MORE OR LESS ABSENT HUSBAND.

I'M SICK OF COOKING FOR HIM, AND I'M SICK OF CLEANING THIS MUSEUM.

SHOPLIFTING?!

I COULD GET AN APARTMENT. I HAVE THE NAME OF A PSYCHOLOGIST.

THERE WAS A CERTAIN SOLEMNITY TO THE MOMENT.

SHOCKING AS ALL THIS WAS TO HEAR, IT WAS THE FIRST TIME MY MOTHER HAD SPOKEN TO ME AS ANOTHER ADULT.

I CAN'T STAND IT ANY MORE. THIS HOUSE IS A TINDERBOX.

Sunbeam RANCH

YOU'VE DONE ENOUGH. YOU SHOULD GO.

EACH DAY OF MY VACATION, I FLED TO THE LOCAL COLLEGE LIBRARY.

AHHH.

I HAD A PAPER TO WRITE FOR MY PHILOSOPHY OF ART CLASS, BUT AGAIN, THE SIRENS CALLED.

HM 701 HN 995

HQ1 HV547

KATE MILLETT APPEARED TO BE A LATTER-DAY COLETTE, WITH THE LIBERTINE ARIS-TOCRATS EXCHANGED FOR CONCEPTUAL ARTISTS AND RADICAL FEMINISTS.

KATE MILLETT

FLYING

EYE-CATCHING SILVER-AND-HOT-PINK COVER

217

I CHECKED THE BOOK OUT, RIVETED BY THE AVALANCHE PACE AND SHAMELESS NAME-DROPPING. LIKE THE SCENE WITH JILL JOHNSTON IN A LONDON PUB.

Jill sits across from me saying there is not enough opportunity for heroism over here. I am late coming into this mean old bar full of Americans. Too early for a martini but I have one anyway. Jill is eating a sandwich. Heroism is suspect, I say. She frankly wants to be heroic. "Admit it, you do too," she says. I do sometimes. Not now. Now it just seems deluded. Because she has said it out loud.

COME HELP ME POLISH THE SILVER.

KATE MILLETT

I'D BEEN WAITING FOR SOME TIME ALONE WITH DAD. I MADE A VALIANT EFFORT TO BROACH THE TOPIC.

I HAD VIEWED THE COMMENT MORE AS AN ENTRY POINT, AND WASN'T REALLY PREPARED TO FOLLOW IT UP.

THE GAY GROUP AT SCHOOL IS PICKETING THAT MOVIE *CRUISING*.

TWINKLE

WHY?

UHH...I DUNNO. I GUESS BECAUSE IT HAS, LIKE, BAD STEREOTYPES.

TWI

I DROPPED THE SUBJECT. PARTLY BECAUSE OF HIS DERISION, BUT MOSTLY BECAUSE OF THE FEAR IN HIS EYES.

AT THE END OF THE WEEK WE WENT TO A MOVIE TOGETHER.

I WAS DETERMINED TO MAKE ANOTHER FORAY.

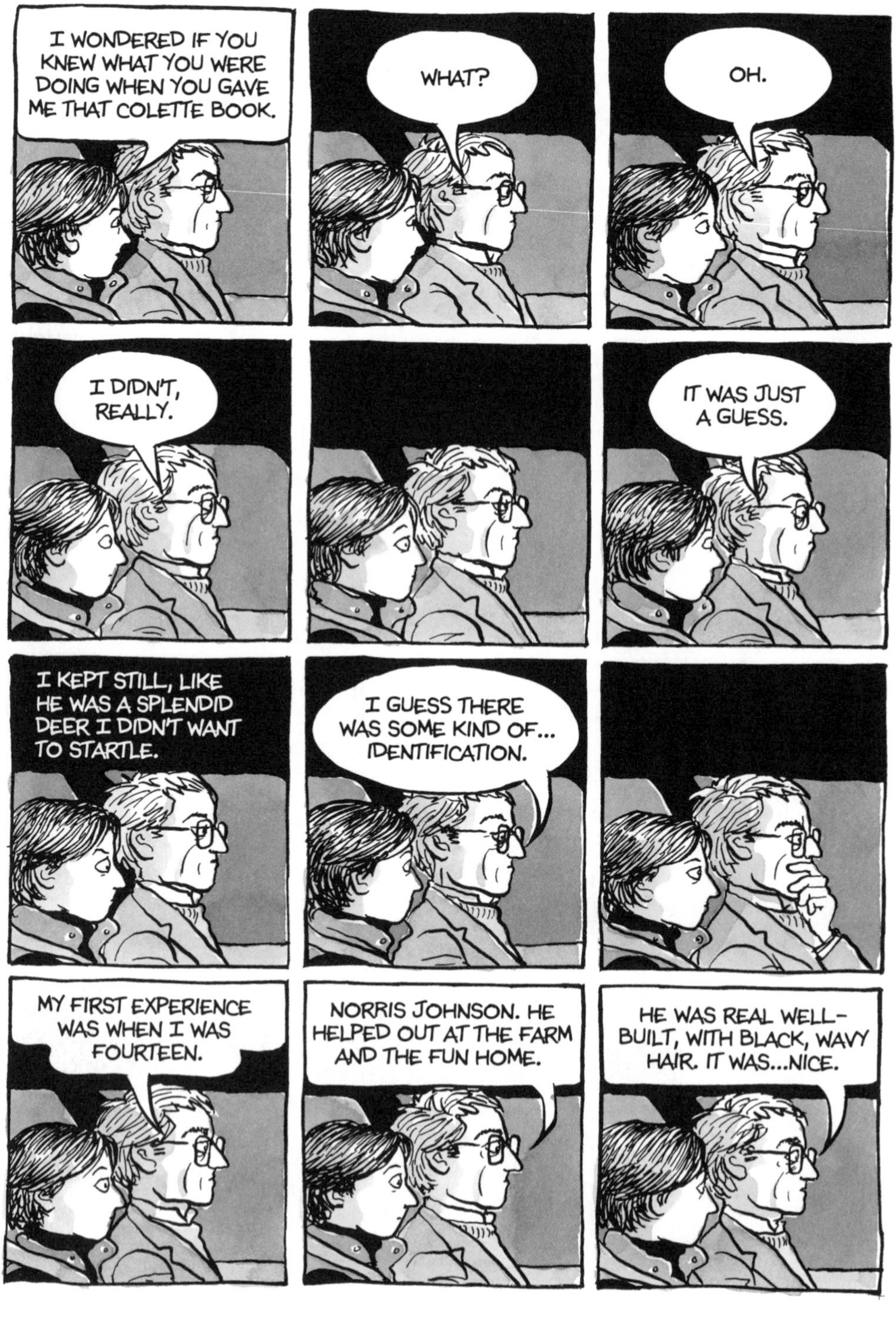
I WONDERED IF YOU KNEW WHAT YOU WERE DOING WHEN YOU GAVE ME THAT COLETTE BOOK.
WHAT?
OH.
I DIDN'T, REALLY.
IT WAS JUST A GUESS.
I KEPT STILL, LIKE HE WAS A SPLENDID DEER I DIDN'T WANT TO STARTLE.
I GUESS THERE WAS SOME KIND OF... IDENTIFICATION.
MY FIRST EXPERIENCE WAS WHEN I WAS FOURTEEN.
NORRIS JOHNSON. HE HELPED OUT AT THE FARM AND THE FUN HOME.
HE WAS REAL WELL-BUILT, WITH BLACK, WAVY HAIR. IT WAS...NICE.

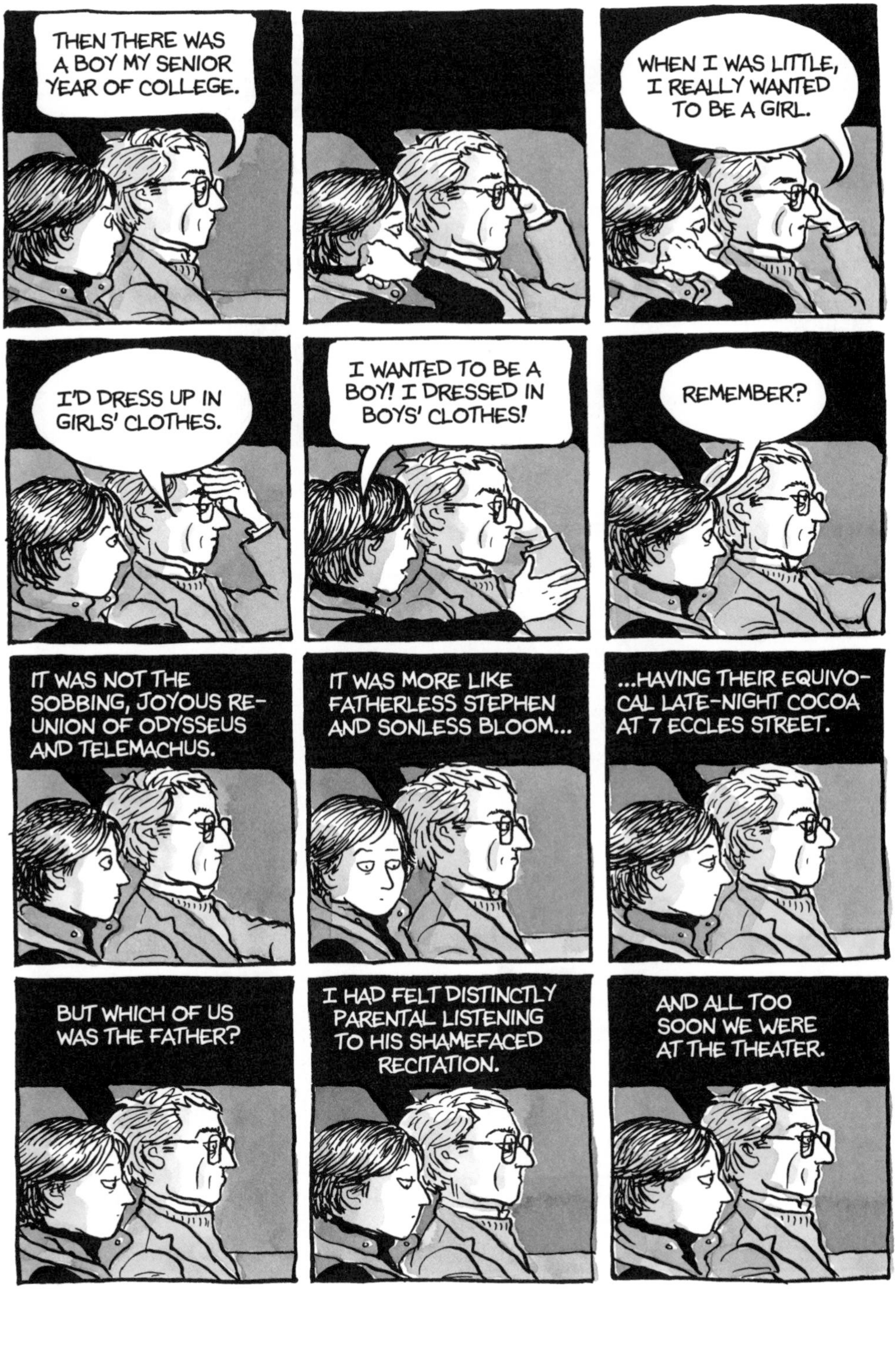
THEN THERE WAS A BOY MY SENIOR YEAR OF COLLEGE.
WHEN I WAS LITTLE, I REALLY WANTED TO BE A GIRL.
I'D DRESS UP IN GIRLS' CLOTHES.
I WANTED TO BE A BOY! I DRESSED IN BOYS' CLOTHES!
REMEMBER?
IT WAS NOT THE SOBBING, JOYOUS RE-UNION OF ODYSSEUS AND TELEMACHUS.
IT WAS MORE LIKE FATHERLESS STEPHEN AND SONLESS BLOOM...
...HAVING THEIR EQUIVO-CAL LATE-NIGHT COCOA AT 7 ECCLES STREET.
BUT WHICH OF US WAS THE FATHER?
I HAD FELT DISTINCTLY PARENTAL LISTENING TO HIS SHAMEFACED RECITATION.
AND ALL TOO SOON WE WERE AT THE THEATER.

THE MOVIE WAS GOOD. IT WAS ABOUT HOW LORETTA LYNN MAKES IT OUT OF APPALACHIA TO BECOME A BIG COUNTRY-WESTERN STAR.

INDEED, DADDY CROAKED OF BLACK LUNG DISEASE A FEW SCENES LATER, BEFORE SHE GOT BACK TO VISIT.

I WOULD SEE MY FATHER ONE MORE TIME AFTER THIS. BUT WE WOULD NEVER DISCUSS OUR SHARED PREDILECTION AGAIN.

Did Bloom discover common factors of similarity between their respective like and unlike reactions to experience?

Both were sensitive to artistic impressions musical in prefer-
preferred a continental to an
tic to a transatlantic place of
rly domestic training and an
resistance professed their dis-
us, national, social and ethical
doctrines. Both admitted the alternately stimulating and obtunding influence of heterosexual magnetism.

obtunding?

WE HAD HAD OUR ITHACA MOMENT.

222

IN OUR CASE, OF COURSE, SUBSTITUTE THE ALTERNATELY STIMULATING AND OBTUNDING INFLUENCE OF HOMOSEXUAL MAGNETISM.

MY-O-MY BAR

Nightly Entertainm̲ 9 P.M. - 2

PARKING IN REA

AFTER THE MOVIE, DAD TOOK ME TO A NOTORIOUS LOCAL NIGHTSPOT. THE FRONT WAS A TOPLESS CLUB. THE BACK WAS A GAY BAR.

THIS MIGHT HAVE BEEN OUR CIRCE CHAPTER, LIKE WHEN STEPHEN AND BLOOM DRINK AT THE BROTHEL IN NIGHTTOWN.

I.D.?

I'M HER FATHER.

TWENTY-ONE, BUD.

OR AT LEAST, IT COULD HAVE BEEN A FUNNY STORY ONE DAY.

AS IT WAS, WE DROVE HOME IN MORTIFIED SILENCE.

I RETURNED TO SCHOOL.

A LETTER FROM DAD FOLLOWED.

"I'M FLYING HIGH ON KATE MILLETT. STARTED READING IT THE DAY YOU LEFT. IT JUST PULLS YOU IN. GOD, WHAT GUTS."

IN AN ELOQUENT UNCONSCIOUS GESTURE, I HAD LEFT *FLYING* FOR HIM TO RETURN TO THE LIBRARY—MIRRORING HIS OWN TROJAN HORSE GIFT OF COLETTE.

> Are there two different worlds? Here and there
> Is there any place they meet? She just did
> the Wellesley commencement. Condemning them as
> ossified matrons with "offspring."
>   Okay, there are three worlds—rich straight,
> poor straight, and then artistic intellectual.
>   I seem the dumbest about the intellectual.
> I've only rubbed elbows with the cultural artistic.
> I see you fitting the mold of this better.
> The values in how and why not things.

"I GUESS I REALLY PREFER MILLETT'S PHILOSOPHY TO THE ONE I'M SLAVE TO. BUT I TRY TO KEEP ONE FOOT IN THE DOOR. ACTUALLY I AM IN LIMBO. I... OH, HELL. I DON'T KNOW WHAT I MEAN."

224

AT THE END OF THE SEMESTER JOAN CAME HOME WITH ME FOR A VISIT. I DID NOT INTRODUCE HER AS MY GIRLFRIEND.

THIS WAS THE LAST TIME I'D SEE DAD.

ON OUR FINAL EVENING, A FAMILY FRIEND REMARKED ADMIRINGLY TO JOAN ON THE CLOSE RELATIONSHIP BETWEEN MY FATHER AND ME.

IT WAS UNUSUAL, AND WE WERE CLOSE. BUT NOT CLOSE ENOUGH.

IN *ULYSSES*, BLOOM RIDES WITH SOME OTHER MEN, INCLUDING STEPHEN'S FATHER, TO A FRIEND'S FUNERAL.

The carriage climbed more slowly the hill of Rutland square. Rattle his bones. Over the stones. Only a pauper. Nobody owns.

— In the midst of life, Martin Cunningham said.

— But the worst of all, Mr Power said, is the man who takes his own life.

Martin Cunningham drew out and put it back.

— The greatest disgrace to hav added.

— Temporary insanity, of cours decisively. We must take a charitable view of it.

— They say a man who does it is a coward, Mr Dedalus said.

— It is not for us to judge, Martin Cunningham said.

Mr Bloom, about to speak, closed his lips again. Martin Cunningham's large eyes. Looking away now. Sympathetic human man he is. Intelligent. Like Shakespeare's face. Always a good word to say. They have no mercy on that here or infanticide. Refuse christian burial. They used to drive a stake of wood through his heart in the grave. As if it wasn't broken already.

> MR. POWER'S THOUGHTLESS REMARKS REMIND BLOOM OF HIS OWN FATHER'S DEATH.

(Bloom's father— suicide)

RUDOLPH BLOOM, NÉE VIRAG, HAD NOT BEEN AS RESILIENT AS HIS SON TO THE STRAIN OF LIFE IN ANTI-SEMITIC DUBLIN.

HE'D TAKEN AN OVERDOSE OF SOMETHING. BUT AT LEAST HE'D LEFT A LETTER. "FOR MY SON LEOPOLD."

DAD LEFT NO NOTE. AFTER THE FUNERAL, LIFE PRETTY MUCH RESUMED ITS COURSE. THEY SAY GRIEF TAKES MANY FORMS, INCLUDING THE ABSENCE OF GRIEF.

IN ONE OF DAD'S COURTSHIP LETTERS TO MOM, HE PRAISES SOMETHING SHE'D WRITTEN IN HER LAST POST BY COMPARING IT TO JAMES JOYCE.

Your first page is better than Joyce...
(except for the line "And he asked me with
his eyes"— which is the best thing ever written—
passion on paper who else could do it?)

down in their little bit of a shop and Ronda with the old
windows of the posadas glancing eyes a lattice hid for her lover
⬛ alf open at night and the
⬛ the boat at Algeciras the
⬛ is lamp and O that awful
⬛ ea crimson sometimes like
⬛ e figtrees in the Alameda
⬛ streets and pink and blue
⬛ ns and the jessamine and
⬛ ar as a girl where I was a
⬛ put the rose in my hair
like the Andalusian girls used or shall I wear a red yes and how
he kissed me under the Moorish wall and I thought well as
well him as another and then I asked him with my eyes to ask
again yes and then he asked me would I yes to say yes my
⬛ t my arms around him yes and
⬛ uld feel my breasts all perfume
⬛ mad and yes I said yes I will Yes.

IN A TELLING MISTAKE, DAD
IMPUTES THE BESEECHING
EYES TO BLOOM INSTEAD
OF TO HIS WIFE, MOLLY.

BUT HOW COULD HE ADMIRE
JOYCE'S LENGTHY, LIBIDINAL
"YES" SO FERVENTLY AND
END UP SAYING "NO" TO HIS
OWN LIFE?

I SUPPOSE THAT A LIFETIME SPENT HIDING
ONE'S EROTIC TRUTH COULD HAVE A CUM-
ULATIVE RENUNCIATORY EFFECT. SEXUAL
SHAME IS IN ITSELF A KIND OF DEATH.

ULYSSES, OF COURSE, WAS BANNED FOR MANY YEARS
BY PEOPLE WHO FOUND ITS HONESTY OBSCENE.

Trieste-Zurich-Paris, 1914-1921.

[THE END]

228

THE FRONT MATTER OF MY MODERN LIBRARY EDITION INCLUDES THE DECISION BY THE JUDGE WHO LIFTED THE BAN IN 1933.

ALONG WITH A LETTER FROM JOYCE TO RANDOM HOUSE, DETAILING *ULYSSES'* PUBLICATION HISTORY TO DATE.

HE MENTIONS THAT MARGARET ANDERSON AND JANE HEAP WERE PROSECUTED FOR RUNNING EPISODES IN THEIR MAGAZINE, THE *LITTLE REVIEW*.

HE ACKNOWLEDGES THE RISK SYLVIA BEACH TOOK IN PUBLISHING A MANU-SCRIPT NO ONE ELSE WOULD TOUCH.

PERHAPS IT'S JUST A COINCIDENCE THAT THESE WOMEN--ALONG WITH SYLVIA'S LOVER ADRIENNE MONNIER, WHO PUBLISHED THE FRENCH EDITION OF *ULYSSES*--WERE ALL LESBIANS.

YOU SHOULD LEARN ABOUT PARIS IN THE TWENTIES, THAT WHOLE SCENE.

BUT I LIKE TO THINK THEY WENT TO THE MAT FOR THIS BOOK *BECAUSE* THEY WERE LESBIANS, BECAUSE THEY KNEW A THING OR TWO ABOUT EROTIC TRUTH.

"EROTIC TRUTH" IS A RATHER SWEEPING CONCEPT.

I SHOULDN'T PRETEND TO KNOW WHAT MY FATHER'S WAS.

PERHAPS MY EAGERNESS TO CLAIM HIM AS "GAY" IN THE WAY I AM "GAY," AS OPPOSED TO BISEXUAL OR SOME OTHER CATEGORY, IS JUST A WAY OF KEEPING HIM TO MYSELF--A SORT OF INVERTED OEDIPAL COMPLEX.

I THINK OF HIS LETTER, THE ONE WHERE HE DOES AND DOESN'T COME OUT TO ME.

Helen just seems to be suggesting that you keep your options open. I tend to go along with that but probably for different reasons. Of course, it seems like a cop out. But then, who are cop outs for? Taking sides is rather heroic, and I am not a hero. What is really worth it?

IT'S EXACTLY THE DISAVOWAL STEPHEN DEDALUS MAKES AT THE BEGINNING OF ULYSSES--JOYCE'S NOD TO THE NOVEL'S MOCK-HEROIC METHOD.

— A woeful lunatic, Mulligan said. Were you in a funk?
— I was, Stephen said with energy and growing fear. Out here in the dark with a man I don't know raving and moaning to himself about shooting a black panther. You saved men from drowning. I'm not a hero, however. If he stays on here I am off.
Buck Mulligan frowned at the lather on his razorblade. He hopped down from his perch and began to search his trousers

IN THE END, JOYCE BROKE HIS CONTRACT WITH BEACH AND SOLD ULYSSES TO RANDOM HOUSE FOR A TIDY SUM.

HE DID NOT OFFER TO REPAY HER FOR THE FINANCIAL SACRIFICES SHE'D MADE FOR HIS BOOK.

BEACH PUT A GOOD FACE ON IT, WRITING "A BABY BELONGS TO ITS MOTHER, NOT TO THE MIDWIFE, DOESN'T IT?"

AND AS LONG AS WE'RE LIKENING *ULYSSES* TO A CHILD, IT FARED MUCH BETTER THAN JOYCE'S ACTUAL CHILDREN.

WENT MAD

BECAME AN ALCOHOLIC

BUT I SUPPOSE THIS IS CONSISTENT WITH THE BOOK'S THEME THAT SPIRITUAL, NOT CONSUBSTANTIAL, PATERNITY IS THE IMPORTANT THING.

IS IT SO UNUSUAL FOR THE TWO THINGS TO COINCIDE?

WHAT IF ICARUS HADN'T HURTLED INTO THE SEA? WHAT IF HE'D INHERITED HIS FATHER'S INVENTIVE BENT? WHAT MIGHT HE HAVE WROUGHT?

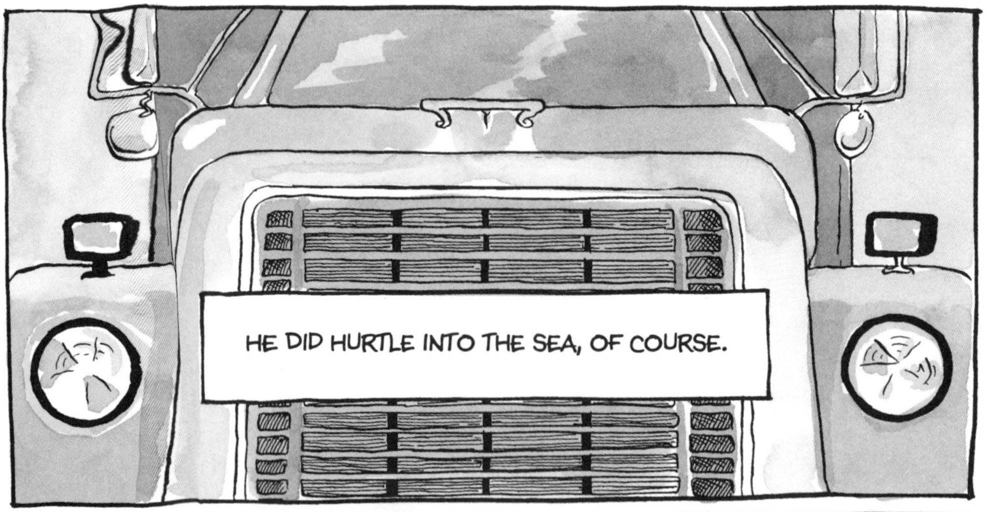
HE DID HURTLE INTO THE SEA, OF COURSE.

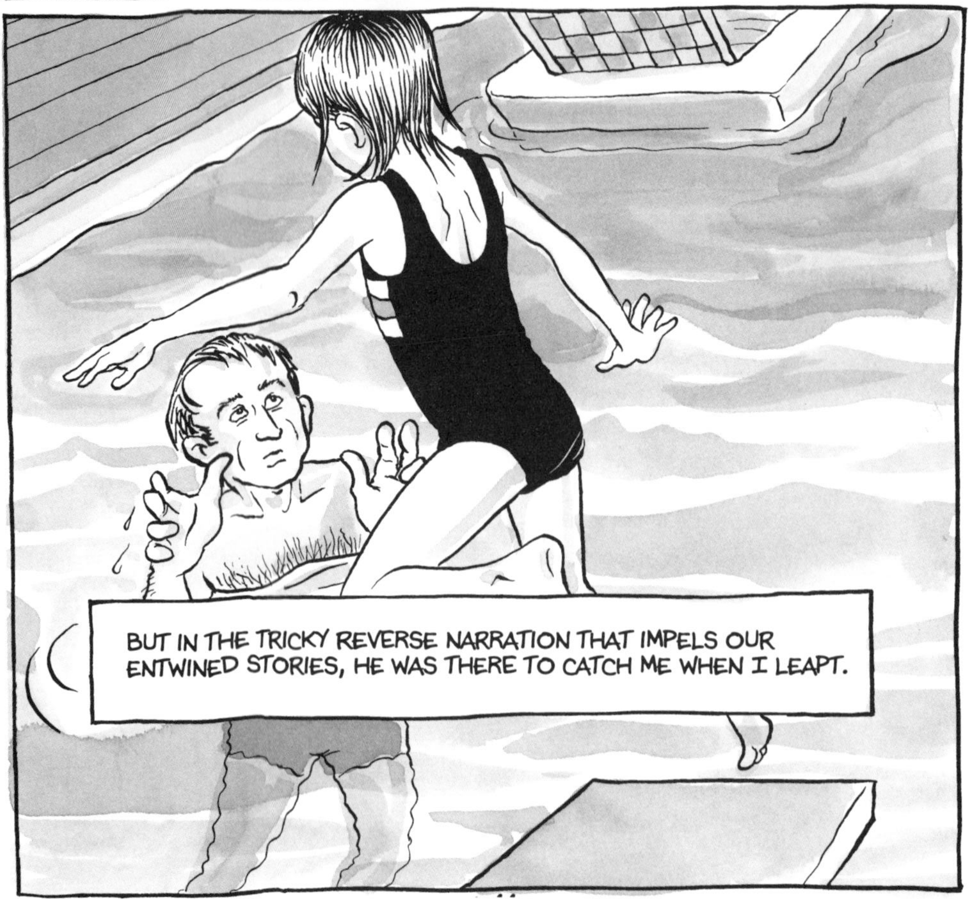
BUT IN THE TRICKY REVERSE NARRATION THAT IMPELS OUR ENTWINED STORIES, HE WAS THERE TO CATCH ME WHEN I LEAPT.

ACKNOWLEDGMENTS

THANKS TO HELEN, CHRISTIAN, AND JOHN BECHDEL FOR NOT TRYING TO STOP ME FROM WRITING THIS BOOK.

I'M VERY GRATEFUL TO LUCY JANE BLEDSOE, HARRIET MALINOWITZ, AND RUTH HOROWITZ FOR READING AND RESPONDING TO EARLY DRAFTS.

I CAN'T POSSIBLY EXPRESS ENOUGH GRATITUDE TO HOWARD CRUSE FOR HIS INSPIRATION AS WELL AS FOR HIS EXTREME GENEROSITY WITH PHOTOSHOP ADVICE AND INSTRUCTION. STEPH SALMON AND KATHY MARMOR HELPED ME TO DIVINE FURTHER MYSTERIES OF PHOTOSHOP AND ILLUSTRATOR. AMEY RADCLIFFE AND SOPHIE HOROWITZ PROVIDED GIMLET-EYED COMPUTER ASSISTANCE AT THE LAST MINUTE.

I'M DEEPLY INDEBTED TO CATHY RESMER FOR HER COMMITTED ADMINISTRATION OF OTHER AREAS OF MY WORK LIFE SO THAT I COULD COMPLETE THIS PROJECT.

THANKS TO DAISY BENSON, DAVID CHRISTENSEN, MAGGIE DESCH, NANCY GOLD-STEIN, TANIA KUPCZAK, JUDITH LEVINE, SAMUEL LURIE, BETTY LYONS, HELEN SCOTT, AND VAL ROHY. THANKS TO JOAN, FOR THE USE OF HER POEM IN CHAPTER THREE.

THANKS TO MY AGENT SYDELLE KRAMER FOR HER HELP SHAPING THE BOOK IN ITS EARLY STAGES. BEING EDITED BY DEANNE URMY WAS A PROFOUND PLEASURE. ANNE CHALMERS WAS A CALMING INFLUENCE THROUGHOUT THE DESIGN AND PRODUCTION PROCESS. THANKS TO MICHAELA SULLIVAN FOR HER COVER CONCEPT, AND BETH FULLER FOR HER RIGOROUS COPY- AND PICTURE-EDITING.

I'M GRATEFUL TO NANCY BEREANO FOR HER EARLY ENCOURAGEMENT TO TELL THIS STORY.

AND TO AMY RUBIN--MY BUDDY, MY SALLY, MY CONSTANT COLLABORATOR-- THANKS SEEMS A FEEBLE OFFERING INDEED, BUT I HOPE YOU'LL TAKE IT.

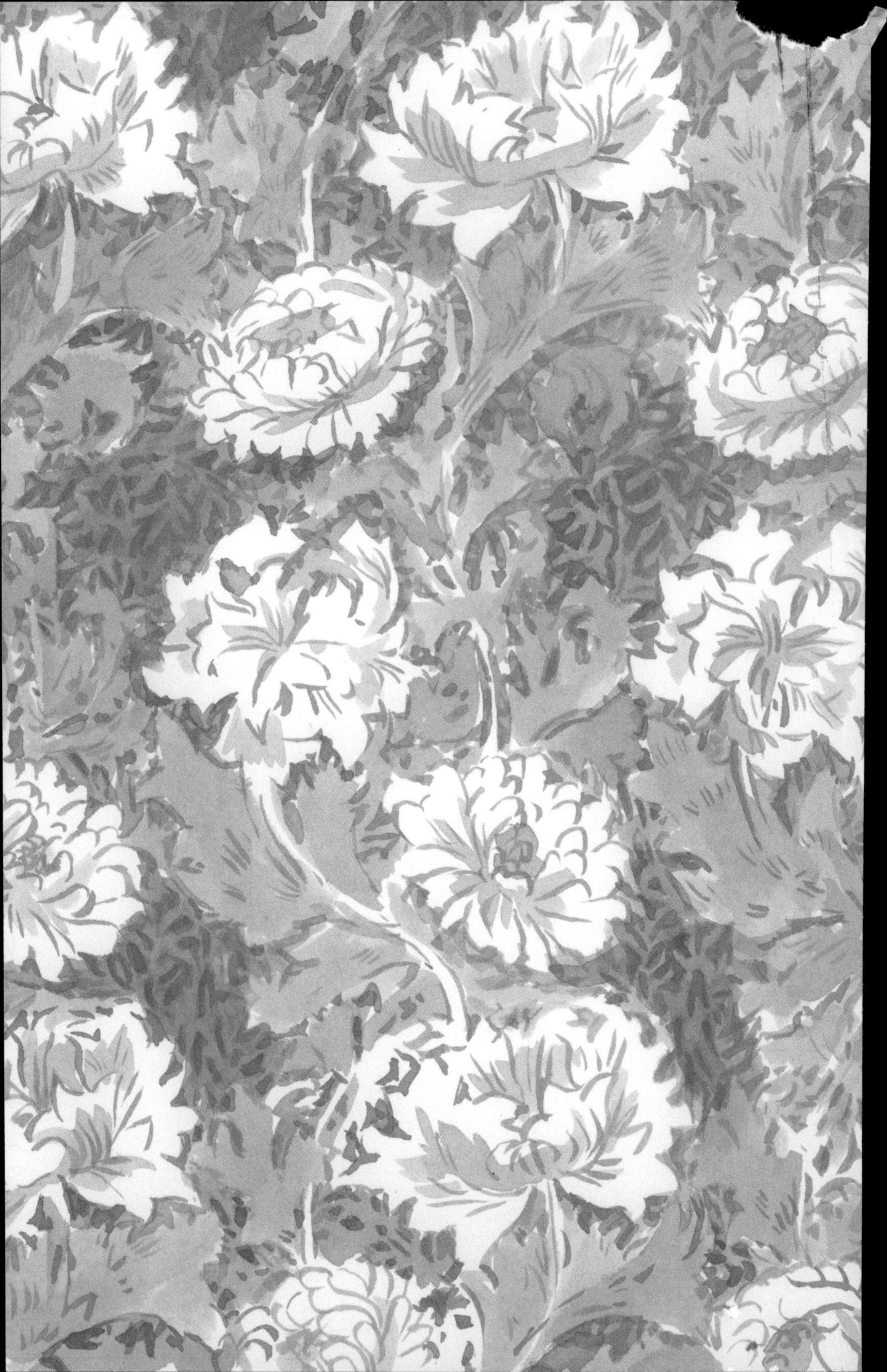